Sushi Cookbook

Quick and Easy Recipes to Make Healthy Sushi at Home

MAGGIE BARTON

SUSHI COOKBOOK

Copyright © 2020 Maggie Barton
All rights reserved.

CONTENTS

INTRODUCTION 7

DIFFERENT TYPES OF SUSHI 7

10 REASONS WHY YOU SHOULD EAT SUSHI MORE OFTEN 8

NUTRIENTS IN SUSHI 10

SUSHI SAUCES 13

SOY SESAME HONEY SAUCE 14

JAPANESE SAUCE 15

TERIYAKI SAUCE 16

SUSHI SAUCE 17

SUSHI RECIPES 18

QUICK SUSHI RICE 19

SUSHI RICE 1 20

TEMAKI 22

SASHIMI ON POINTED CABBAGE SALAD 24

NIGIRI 26

SAKE NIGIRI (SALMON) 28

EBI NIGIRI (SHRIMPS) 30

NIGIRI (SMOKED SALMON) 32

SURIMI MAKI 33

SAKE MAKI (SALMON) 34

TEKKA MAKI (TUNA) 36

KIMCHI MAKI 38

SUSHI ROLLS 40

THIN SUSHI ROLLS 42

THICK SUSHI ROLLS 44

MUSHROOM SUSHI ROLLS 46

FISH AND CHIPS SUSHI ROLLS 48

BUCKWHEAT SUSHI ROLLS 50

CRISPY BIG SUSHI ROLLS 52

CAULIFLOWER SUSHI ROLLS 54

EGG SUSHI ROLLS 56

VEGAN SUSHI ROLLS 58

VEGAN SUSHI DELUXE 60

VEGAN SPICY SUSHI ROLLS 62

VEGETABLE SUSHI ROLLS 64

VEGETABLE SUSHI MIX 66

CHEESE SUSHI ROLLS 68

TOFU SUSHI ROLLS 69

AVOCADO SUSHI ROLLS 70

SHIITAKE MUSHROOMS FOR SUSHI ROLLS 72

SHIITAKE SUSHI ROLLS 74

CAPRESE SUSHI ROLLS 75

HERBAL MUSHROOM SUSHI ROLLS 76

CARROT AND CUCUMBER SUSHI ROLLS 78

SUSHI WITH CAULIFLOWER 80

CALIFORNIA ROLLS 82

CALIFORNIA ROLLS - SALMON AND AVOCADO 84

CALIFORNIA ROLLS INSIDE OUT 86

CALIFORNIA SUSHI WRAPS 88

SUSHI MIX 1 90

SUSHI MIX 2 93

SUSHI MIX 3 96

SUSHI BURRITO WITH TURKEY, MANGO AND AVOCADO 98

SUSHI BALLS 100

CUCUMBER SUSHI 102

DITHMARSCHER SUSHI 104

OSHI SUSHI 106

SUSHI SANDWICH 108

VEGGIE ONIGIRI 110

ONIGIRI WITH SALMON AND CHICKEN 112

TOAST SUSHI ROLLS 114

TOAST ROLLS WITH SALMON CREAM CHEESE FILLING 116

DISHES 117

TUNA TARTARE ON AVOCADO CREAM 118

SPICY TUNA TARTARE 120

TUNA TARTARE WITH CORIANDER PESTO 122

REFINED TUNA TARTARE 124

SALMON TARTARE WITH LEMON CREAM 126

TUNA CARPACCIO 128

HAND CHEESE 129

PANGASIUS ON FENNEL SALAD IN ORANGE VINAIGRETTE 130

MARINATED TUNA ON A NORI AND RICE BED 132

ASIAN COLESLAW WITH GLAZED SALMON FILLET 134

SIMPLE POKE BOWL 136

TAMAGOYAKI SUSHI OMELETTE 138

INARI SUSHI 140

SUSHI PATTIES 142

VEGAN GOLUBTSI ON BRAISED VEGETABLES 144

SUSHI BOWL 146

JAPANESE SEAWEED SALAD 148

SUSHI SALAD 150

JAPANESE ONION SAUCE WITH CABBAGE AND SHRIMP 152

PASTA SALAD WITH ROASTED BROCCOLI AND PEANUT-SILK TOFU SAUCE 154

SUSHI BOWL WITH TAMAGOYAKI 156

BEEF WITH ONIONS AND SUGAR SNAP PEAS FROM THE WOK 158

SASHIMI BOWL 160

POKÉ BOWL 162

JAPANESE STYLE BOWL 164

BBQ ROLLS 166

ASIAN FISH BALLS 168

DESSERT 169

SUSHI WITH A DIFFERENCE - SWEET AS A DESSERT 170

SWEET SUSHI 172

SWEET SUSHI WITH FRUITS 174

RICE PUDDING 176

BANANA MAKI SUSHI 178

SUMMER SUSHI 179

SUSHI CAKE 180

CUCUMBER SUSHI 182

INTRODUCTION

The Japanese sushi dish has never been more popular than it is now. Previously it was often eaten as a side dish in other restaurants, but nowadays there are numerous specialized sushi restaurants. You can now also find sushi in supermarkets in all kinds of different shapes. Sushi is popular for a good reason, because it is not only tasty, but also healthy. The main ingredients of sushi, rice, fish and vegetables are all considered healthy as they contain many different vitamins. In addition, sushi is easy to digest and made from fresh products.

Thanks to the fresh vegetables used to make sushi, you get your much needed antioxidants and the fish provides your daily vitamins and minerals. Not only the sushi itself is healthy, the soy sauce also has health benefits. Soy is good for your bones and circulation and wasabi has an antibacterial effect. Sushi has many health benefits, but of course it depends on how you eat sushi. If you choose to make sushi yourself, make sure that the fish you use is safe to eat raw. For Healthy sushi, it is better to leave out the fat dips and use the soy sauce sparingly. In short, sushi can be a very healthy and tasty meal, but pay attention to how big your portion is and how many extras you put on your rice rolls.

DIFFERENT TYPES OF SUSHI

NIGIRI SUSHI

Nigiri Sushi consists of a small portion of sticky rice, which is shaped with the hands. Depending on the type of sushi, a piece of fish (salmon, tuna) or vegetables is placed on it. Depending on your taste, you can also combine it with wasabi paste.

MAKI-SUSHI

In Maki-Sushi the rice is wrapped in dried seaweed (nori). For this you need a bamboo mat. Salmon, shrimp or tuna are best suited for the filling. You can also incorporate cucumber sticks, carrot sticks or spring onions.

TEMAKI-SUSHI

In contrast to Nigiri-Sushi, Temaki-Sushi is more like a school bag. The rice is also packed in nori, but the algae leaf is rolled up conically. In addition, the typical sushi ingredients such as fish (shrimp, salmon) and vegetables are used again.

CALIFORNIA ROLLS

California rolls are less common in Japan, but are very popular in Europe. The basic ingredients are similar to maki sushi, but are processed the other way round. The nori sheets are inside, the rice outside. Some sesame seeds or salmon roe decorate this sushi variant.

10 REASONS WHY YOU SHOULD EAT SUSHI MORE OFTEN

1. SUSHI COMES IN A LOT OF VARIATIONS

There are a lot of different types of sushi. So there will always be a sushi that you appreciate. Moreover, eating sushi will not get bored that way. Every time you put a different variant on your plate.

2. SUSHI IS HEALTHY

Sushi is known as a healthy food. After all, it is prepared with various fresh fish, vegetables, so full of vitamins, and rice. If you are a fan of vegetarian food, there are still the countless veggie variants with only delicious vegetables. This means that even if you are a vegetarian, you can enjoy sushi.

3. SUSHI IS EASY TO DIGEST

The ingredients that sushi is made of make this an easily digestible meal. Because sushi is not heavy on your stomach, it is an excellent meal to eat at noon. So replace your lunch with sushi and make it something special, but also very tasty. Of course this also applies if you replace your dinner with different types of sushi, because even then the meal will be easy to digest and very tasty. Fortunately, after eating, sometimes even huge amounts of sushi, the annoying bloating does not occur. So you can always put sushi on the menu.

4. EATING SUSHI IS FUN

Eating sushi is an excellent way to enjoy yourself with your loved ones. After all, enjoying different delicious sushi variants together is very pleasant. Moreover, there will usually be laughed a lot. Eating sushi with chopsticks will undoubtedly create laughable situations that will certainly enhance the atmosphere at the table. Once you've eaten sushi, look forward to your next sushi date.

5. SUSHI IS ALWAYS FRESH FOOD

Because only fresh ingredients are used for the preparation of sushi, you can be sure that no nutrients will be lost. You are also sure that you do not receive products that have passed the expiry date. In most restaurants where sushi is on the menu, these delicious snacks are almost made in front of you. Because the preparation is very fast, you will never have to wait long before you can enjoy.

6. SUSHI IS A FEAST FOR THE EYES

When you eat, the eye wants something. For that reason, sushi is ideal to put on the table. The presentation of these delicious snacks is often done in a very beautiful and creative way. You can think of sushi that is brought to the table in the form of a boat. Almost a shame to eat, but also too tasty to leave.

7. YOU CAN ALSO PREPARE SUSHI AT HOME

While many great sushi restaurants exist, you can also choose to prepare these treats at home. The preparation of sushi is not really difficult because you hardly have to cook (only the rice). After preparing sushi, your kitchen doesn't have to look like a pigsty. You also don't have to toil for hours in the kitchen before you can finally get to the table.

8. PREPARING SUSHI CANNOT GO WRONG

The preparation of sushi can hardly go wrong because you don't have to bake anything. Therefore, no products can burn, so your meal will end up in the trash. You do not have to be a kitchen prince or princess to serve a delicious sushi meal to your family and friends. In addition, there are special sushi kits on the market that contain everything you have left for preparing a sushi meal. Of course, such a kit also contains all the information you need to prepare the dishes.

9. SUSHI IS ALSO DELIVERED AT HOME

When you don't feel like going to a sushi restaurant, but don't want to prepare these tasty snacks yourself, there are also companies that deliver the desired sushi at home. In recent years, these companies have sprung up all over the country like mushrooms. So there will probably be one in your area. You no longer even have to leave your home to eat tasty sushi, just order and pay by phone or via the internet, and the goodies will be delivered to any desired address within seconds.

10. SUSHI BOWL IS ALSO POSSIBLE

If you want to serve sushi to your guests in a special way, you can also choose to make a sushi bowl. For this you only have to put the desired ingredients in a bowl. So you don't have to roll sushi. This is perhaps the simplest way to enjoy sushi. You can make a sushi bowl almost anywhere, anytime.

NUTRIENTS IN SUSHI

Many sushi lovers would not hesitate to put the stamp "healthy" on Asian finger food. But is sushi really healthy? To clarify this question, we have to take a closer look at the different components of rice rolls and their ingredients:

RAW FISH

The typical main ingredients for sushi are raw fish or seafood, including, for example, tuna, salmon, freshwater eel, mackerel, shrimp and crab meat. These sea creatures are rich in high-quality animal protein, which humans need for various metabolic processes and building up the body's own proteins.
Iodine, a component of thyroid hormones, and some vitamins are also included. So fish is one of the main dietary sources of vitamin D. Mackerel and salmon in particular can have a high vitamin D content.
Fish is also an important supplier of omega-3 fatty acids: the fatty acids are present in high concentrations in the brain and nerve cells and reduce the risk of cardiovascular diseases.

RICE

White rice grains are used in combination with a vinegar mixture, sugar and salt to prepare sushi rice. White rice is the grain that was ground and polished after harvesting - but it hardly contains any vitamins, minerals and fiber.
Since white rice is easier and faster to digest than, for example, brown rice, the blood sugar level rises rapidly after consumption and drops again just as quickly - cravings can be the result. Refined carbohydrates, such as white rice, are suspected of increasing the risk of type 2 diabetes or heart problems.

NORI SHEETS

Hardly any sushi roll can do without nori algae. They keep the delicious filling together and are full of important nutrients. In addition to vitamins A, C, E and B 12, nori sheets provide zinc and some iodine.

They are also fat-free and rich in protein and satiating fiber. Their ingredients can lower blood cholesterol and have an anti-carcinogenic effect.

But if you now hope for a real nutrient bomb, you're wrong: Only a small amount of the algae is needed and processed for the delicious sushi specialties. For an adequate nutrient supply, the rice rolls alone play only a subordinate role.

SOY SAUCE

Maki, nigiri and sashimi are dipped in soy sauce. For sushi fans, however, it is important to know that the traditionally produced soy sauce contains valuable ingredients: it contains certain amino acids and a lot of protein, but only a few calories and no fat.

US researchers also found that dark soy sauce contains about ten times as many antioxidants as red wine. To use this effect, one would have to drink soy sauce by the glass - the usual consumption amounts are hardly sufficient to bring verifiable health benefits.

Some experts also warn that one should think of the salt content in soy sauce, which averages 13 percent. As a natural seasoning, soy sauce is definitely more recommended and healthier than pure salt.

WASABI

Without this hot and green spice, almost nothing works in Japan: wasabi. Incidentally, the widely used term "Japanese horseradish" is wrong: botanically speaking, there is no relationship between horseradish and wasabi.

In addition to the dried leaves, the root of the plant is mainly used to make the popular paste. The mustard oil glycosides, which are abundant in the wasabi, are among the phytochemicals that lower the risk of cancer and have an antibacterial and anti-inflammatory effect.

SUSHI SAUCES

SOY SESAME HONEY SAUCE

INGREDIENTS FOR 1 PORTIONS

- 4 tbsp of soy sauce
- 1 teaspoon of sesame
- 1 teaspoon of honey, liquid

PREPARATION

Total time approx. 2 minutes

1. Mix all the ingredients together and taste best according to your personal needs.

JAPANESE SAUCE

INGREDIENTS FOR 2 PORTIONS

- 1 teaspoon of olive oil
- 1 small onion
- 3 toes garlic
- 10 g of ginger, fresh
- 50 ml soy sauce
- 80 g sugar

PREPARATION

Total time approx. 10 minutes

1. Peel the onion and cut it into small cubes. Peel the garlic and ginger and also finely dice. Fry everything together in the heated olive oil until everything is golden yellow. Add soy sauce and sugar and simmer for another 5-7 minutes. Finally, filter the sauce and only use the pure sauce.

TERIYAKI SAUCE

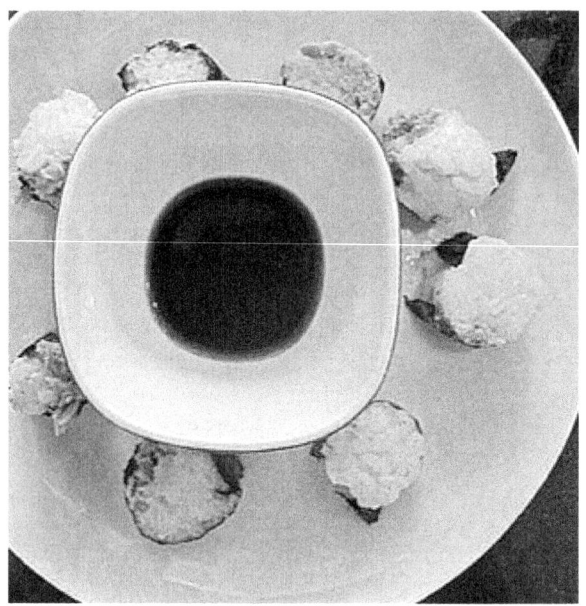

INGREDIENTS FOR 1 PORTIONS

- 4 tbsp. of soy sauce
- 1 tbsp. of rice wine
- Garlic cloves
- 2 teaspoons of ginger, grated
- 1 teaspoon of salt

PREPARATION

Total time approx. 10 minutes

1. Mix all ingredients, garlic pressed, well.
2. This sauce is well suited for marinating meat (recipe information is sufficient for approx. 500 g).
3. Instead of rice wine, sherry can also be used.

SUSHI SAUCE

INGREDIENTS FOR 1 PORTIONS

- 3 tbsp. of soy sauce, dark
- 3 tbsp. of vinegar (sushi - vinegar)
- 4 tbsp. of water
- 1 tbsp. of sugar
- 1 pinch of salt
- 5 drops of oil (sesame oil)
- 0.33 g of bell pepper, red

PREPARATION

Total time approx. 15 minutes

1. Put all other ingredients apart from the peppers in a high container and whisk. Clean the peppers, cut them into very small cubes and add them. Stir again and let steep for a few hours until ready to eat.

SUSHI RECIPES

QUICK SUSHI RICE

INGREDIENTS FOR 4 PORTIONS

- 250 g of rice (sushi - rice)
- 2 tbsp of vinegar (rice vinegar)
- 1 tbsp of sugar
- 1 teaspoon of salt

PREPARATION

Total time approx. 20 minutes

1. Rinse sushi rice in a colander under running cold water until the water runs clear and let the kernels drain well.
2. Bring the rice to the boil with 300 ml of water, let it boil for 2 minutes, reduce the heat and cover and let the rice swell over low heat for 10 minutes.
3. Remove the lid, clamp 2 layers of kitchen paper between the pot and lid and let the rice cool for another 10 to 15 minutes.
4. In the meantime, bring rice vinegar, salt and sugar to the boil and let them cool down again.
5. Put the rice in a bowl, drizzle the vinegar over it and work in with a wooden spatula, but do not stir.
6. Cover the rice with a damp cloth until further use.

SUSHI RICE

INGREDIENTS FOR 4 PORTIONS

- 450 g of rice, california short grain rice (nishiki)
- 600 ml of water

Also: (for the spice mix for sushi rice)

- 100 ml of rice vinegar
- 2 tbsp of sugar
- 1 teaspoon of salt
- 4 drops of soy sauce

PREPARATION

Total time approx. 1 hour 25 minutes

1. Wash rice thoroughly in a sieve until the water remains clear, then drain well.

2. Put the rice with the specified amount of water in the pot and let it rest for about 20 minutes.

3. Then close the pot with a well-fitting lid and slowly warm the contents. Then set the heat to the highest level and bring to a boil.

4. Now put it back on the smallest setting and let the rice swell for about 10 minutes.

5. Take the pot off the stove, put a folded kitchen towel under the lid and let the rice swell for another 10 minutes.

6. Mix the seasoning ingredients in a saucepan and heat until the sugar and salt have completely dissolved.

7. Then pour the seasoning mixture over the rice and mix together. (Warning, there is now rice vinegar that has already been seasoned with salt and sugar, then simply pour the "finished" vinegar over the rice with a dash of soy sauce!)

8. Let the rice cool well. The rice can then be processed into sushi. If the rice is only processed later, it is advisable to cover it with a damp cloth so that it does not dry out.

TEMAKI

INGREDIENTS FOR 1 PORTIONS

- Rice, sushi finished
- 2 nori sheets
- Wasabi paste
- 2 tbsp of rice vinegar
- 250 ml of water

For the filling:

- 2 carrots cut into fine strips
- 1 cucumber, cut into fine strips
- 200 g of salmon, cut into thin strips
- 200 g of tuna cut into thin strips
- 1 pack of surimi, cut into short sticks
- Cress
- Soy sauce
- Ginger pickled

PREPARATION

Total time approx. 30 minutes

1. Mix vinegar and water in a small bowl.

2. Halve a nori sheet in the middle.

3. Immerse your hands in the vinegar water so that the rice does not stick to it.

4. Put a heaped tablespoon of sushi rice in the left half of the seaweed leaf. Spread the rice and spread a little wasabi paste on it.

5. Arrange different fillings diagonally on the rice. They should point to the top left corner of the Nori sheet.

6. Fold the lower left corner to the upper right corner of the nori sheet. Roll up the sheet further into a bag. Glue a grain of rice in the bottom right corner and fasten the corner to the bag.

7. Arrange several sushi bags in a glass or bowl and serve with soy sauce and pickled ginger.

SASHIMI ON POINTED CABBAGE SALAD

INGREDIENTS FOR 4 PORTIONS

- 400 g of salmon, or sushi-quality tuna
- 1 small head of pointed cabbage, about 300g
- Spring onion
- 3 tsp of ginger, pickled sushi
- 1 ½ m in size lemon, the juice
- ½ lemon, cut into 4 slices
- 2 teaspoons of sesame oil
- 4 tsp of soy sauce, light
- 3 tsp of horseradish
- 1 teaspoon of honey
- Salt and pepper
- 2 discs of toast
- 4 tsp of caviar, (trout caviar)
- 2 tbsp of sesame
- 2 tbsp of butter
- Wasabi paste

PREPARATION

Total time approx. 2 hours

1. First grate the cabbage roughly and remove the stalk if necessary. Then cut the spring onions into very fine rings and mix with the grated cabbage.

2. Now cut 3 heaped teaspoons of sushi ginger into small pieces and add them to pointed cabbage.

3. The dressing for the pointed cabbage salad is mixed from the lemon juice, the sesame oil, the soy sauce, the horseradish and the bee honey and added about 1 hour before consumption.

4. Now 2 slices of toast are cut into small cubes and toasted with the butter until golden brown.

5. At the same time, the sesame seeds are roasted in a coated pan (without additives).

6. Shortly before serving, you should season the cabbage salad with salt and pepper. It should have a good sour note and a strong horseradish aroma.

7. Now put one serving of salad (a small cup full) per person on the middle of the plate. Each portion is topped with about 100 g of salmon or tuna in thin strips. As a decorative "crown", place a teaspoon of trout caviar on the pointed cabbage sashimi portion and frame it with the toasted bread cubes. Now only sprinkle the raw fish with the roasted sesame seeds and add a slice of lemon with a dab of wasabi paste and serve immediately.

NIGIRI

INGREDIENTS FOR 1 PORTIONS

- 1 port. of rice, sushi finished
- Wasabi paste
- 200 g of salmon, cut into thin strips
- 200 g of tuna cut into thin strips
- Mackerel, cut into thin strips
- Radish, japanese, pickled
- Rice vinegar
- Water
- Soy sauce
- Pickled ginger

PREPARATION

Total time approx. 30 minutes

1. Mix vinegar and water in a small bowl and dip your hands in it so that the rice does not stick to them.

2. Roll a chicken-sized amount of rice between your palms to create an oval. Place on the work surface and make several such rice balls. Place the toppings in front of the rice balls and spread a little wasabi paste on each rice ball.

3. Place the topping on the rice oval and press down gently.

4. Arrange on a plate and serve with soy sauce and pickled ginger.

SAKE NIGIRI (SALMON)

INGREDIENTS FOR 1 PORTIONS

- 1 cup of rice, (sushi rice)
- 200 g of sliced salmon (wild salmon, smoked)
- 200 g of cream cheese, with herbs
- 1 bunch radish
- 1 tbsp of soy sauce, (light)
- 1 tbsp of sugar
- ½ tsp of salt

For the set:
- Dill flags
- Chives - stalks

PREPARATION

Total time approx. 20 minutes

1. The ingredients are enough for 12 salmon rolls.

2. Cook the rice according to the package, stirring in salt, sugar and soy sauce and then set aside.

3. Clean, wash and finely chop the radishes.

4. Spread the salmon slices slightly overlapping on a work surface covered with foil so that a closed rectangle of approx. 30 x 22 cm is created. Then spread the rice, then the cream cheese on top. Sprinkle the radishes over it and roll up the salmon with the foil and place in the freezer for about 30 minutes.

5. Then take out, cut into approx. 2 cm wide slices, arrange on a plate and garnish with dill flags and chives.

EBI NIGIRI (SHRIMPS)

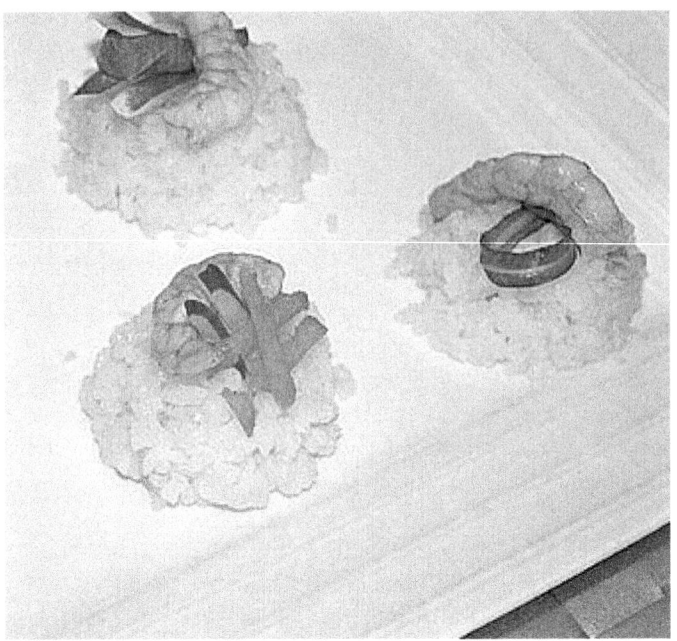

INGREDIENTS FOR 4 PORTIONS

- Rice (sushi - rice), recipe in my profile, half of it
- 8 shrimps - raw, unpeeled tails
- 2 teaspoons of horseradish (wasabi powder)
- 4 tablespoons of water
- 2 tbsp of vinegar (rice vinegar)
- 2 teaspoons of rice wine (mirin)
- Salt
- Soy sauce
- Ginger pickled

PREPARATION

Total time approx. 35 minutes

1. Wash the prawn tails and cook over low heat in boiling salted water for 4 to 5 minutes. Take out and quench in ice water.

2. Mix the wasabi powder with 2-4 tablespoons of water and let it swell. Remove the prawns from the shells, except for the tail segment. Remove the dark intestine from the back. Slit open from the abdomen, but not completely. They should be connected by about 1 cm on each side.

3. Mix rice vinegar and rice wine in a deep plate, turn the prawns inside and let them steep for 2 minutes. Lift out, dab lightly and bend the two halves into a ring. Coat the inside with wafer-thin wasabi paste.

4. With moistened hands, shape 1 tablespoon of sushi rice into an elongated dumpling and press the top slightly flat. Place the prawns on the rice pillows and gently press them down. Press on the sushi with the shrimps.

5. Serve with soy sauce, remaining wasabi paste for dipping and pickled ginger.

NIGIRI (SMOKED SALMON)

INGREDIENTS FOR 4 PORTIONS

- 420 g of rice (sushi rice)
- 300 g of smoked salmon
- Spice paste (wasabi)
- Soy sauce
- Ginger, sweet and sour

PREPARATION

Total time approx. 10 minutes

1. For those who don't really like raw fish. The preparation for sushi rice can be found in the CK database.

2. Cut the salmon into 5 cm long and 3 cm wide strips, dampen hands with water and take about 2 tablespoons of sushi rice and shape them into a 5-6 cm long, rectangular block with rounded sides and corners. Then cover the rice with the salmon strips and shape everything appetizing again.

3. Mix the soy sauce with the wasabi paste (caution spicy) according to taste, add ginger.

SURIMI MAKI

INGREDIENTS FOR 2 PORTIONS

- 1 port of rice (sushi rice), prepared
- 1 pack of surimi
- ½ avocado
- 2 tbsp of cream cheese
- Nori sheets

PREPARATION

Total time approx. 30 minutes

1. Core and peel the avocado, then cut long strips, about 5 x 5 mm thin. Halve or quarter the surimi, depending on the size.
2. Place the nori sheet on a bamboo mat so that the lower side of the nori sheet lies on the lower edge of the mat. Spread the rice about 7mm thick over 2/3 of the nori sheet. Now spread a tablespoon of cream cheese about 3 cm wide in the middle of the rice. Place the avocado and surimi strips on each, about 3 to 4 strips each. Then carefully roll up with even pressure. This results in pretty thick maki rolls. Brush the roll with a little water or rice vinegar / water mixture (this makes it easier to cut). Cut off the ends, cut the roll into pleasant pieces, at least 1.5 cm long.

SAKE MAKI (SALMON)

INGREDIENTS FOR 2 PORTIONS

- 250 g of rice (sushi rice)
- 375 ml of water
- 1 tbsp of rice vinegar
- ½ tbsp of mirin
- ½ tbsp of sugar
- 1 teaspoon of salt
- 6 nori sheets
- 250 g of salmon steak, in the pan from both sides for 8 min. Fried and cut into strips
- 1 teaspoon of wasabi paste
- 6 cm salad cucumber, with skin, cut into thin strips
- ½ bell pepper, red, cut into thin strips

PREPARATION

Total time approx. 45 minutes

1. Wash the rice in a sieve under running water until the draining water is clear. Bring the rice to a boil with the water in a saucepan, reduce the heat considerably and cook the rice for 10-12 minutes. In the meantime, mix the rice vinegar with mirin, sugar and salt in a small bowl until everything is completely dissolved. Put the rice in a flat bowl (no metal!) And let it cool for 10 minutes. Add the rice vinegar solution and carefully fold in with a wooden spoon. Let cool completely and divide into 6 equal portions.

2. Now place a nori sheet with the glossy side down on a bamboo mat and spread 1 rice portion thinly and evenly on it; Leave a 1.5 cm margin at one end. Use a spoon to make a furrow in the front third across the direction of the roll and apply wasabi paste. Be careful, wasabi is pretty hot! Then put the fried salmon strips in the furrow and place cucumber strips and / or pepper strips behind them as you like. Moisten the free end of the nori sheet with a little water. Now raise the bamboo mat at the front a little and lift the nori sheet around the filling under gentle pressure. Raise the bamboo mat further while rolling in the sushi roll until it is completely closed. You have to practice that a couple of times. For me it worked quite well the first time!

3. In the end there are 6 pretty sushi rolls in front of you, waiting for the final maki shape. Now it's time to prepare the tool, meaning to make a good knife ultra-sharp. Otherwise the maki sushi look more like car tires! Place a sushi roll on a wooden board and cut the ends clean straight (the remains are for the cook!). Always immerse the knife in cold water before each further cutting! Divide the sushi roll in the middle and cut each half into 4 equal maki sushi. Arrange on a large plate with the cut surface facing up. Cool the finished sushi or consume it immediately.

4. Set the table, prepare sushi sashimi sauce, wasabi paste and pickled ginger and enjoy piece by piece!

TEKKA MAKI (TUNA)

INGREDIENTS FOR 1 PORTIONS

- 1 can of tuna in water
- 5 tbsp of mayonnaise
- Salt
- Pepper
- Nori sheets
- 100 g of rice, (sushi rice)
- Sugar
- Rice wine

PREPARATION

Total time approx. 1 hour

1. Wash out the sushi rice. This means running water over it until only clear water is left.

2. Then cook according to the package instructions. Put 1/2 teaspoon of sugar in 2 tablespoons of rice wine vinegar and heat. Stir the warm vinegar slowly under the still warm, cooked rice.

3. Mix the tuna with the mayo and salt and pepper and season to taste.

4. For the tuna sushi, place a nori sheet (with the smooth side) on a bamboo mat and spread the adhesive rice thinly on it so that approx. 3/4 of the sheet is covered with rice. A small margin should be left at the top and bottom. In the middle comes a narrow strip with the prepared tuna.

5. Roll everything up and put in the fridge for a few minutes. Then cut the sushi roll and sushi pieces with a lightly dampened and sharp knife.

6. Ginger, wasabi and teriyaki sauce can also be served.

KIMCHI MAKI

INGREDIENTS FOR 3 PORTIONS

- 100 ml of sushi rice
- 1 tbsp of sesame oil, dark
- 1 tbsp of rice vinegar
- 1 tbsp of sesame
- 1 teaspoon of salt
- Spring onion, green part
- 1 pack of nori sheets
- 6 tbsp of kimchi

PREPARATION

Total time approx. 1 hour 5 minutes

1. Cook the rice with double the amount of water over medium heat. Add a little more water if necessary. Let the rice cool and then stir in the sesame oil, rice vinegar, sesame seeds and salt.

2. Spread 2 tablespoons of rice on the lower half of the nori leaf and add a row of spring onions and 2 tablespoons of kimchi. Roll up and dampen the end with water to make it stick better.

3. Place the sushi roll with the seam facing down on a wooden board. Do the same with the other two Nori sheets. Finally cut the rolls into 1.5 - 2 cm thick slices and serve with a little soy sauce.

SUSHI ROLLS

INGREDIENTS FOR 2 PORTIONS

- 1 cup of rice (sushi rice)
- Horseradish (wasabi)
- Nori sheets
- Carrot
- 100 g of meat from crayfish
- 100 g of shrimp
- Salmon, pickled
- Soy sauce
- Pickled ginger
- Spring onions

PREPARATION

Total time approx. 1 hour 30 minutes

1. Soak the sushi rice in the water for about 15 minutes, then let it boil. For a cup of rice you need about 1.5 cups of water. There is also precise instructions on the rice pack.

2. In the meantime, the shrimps can be prepared using a steam cooker and briefly scalding. Peel the carrots and cut them into thin strips. The same goes for the spring onions.

3. Now place one of the nori sheets on a kitchen towel and apply the rice, which has now cooled down, 1 cm from the edge. Cover the leaf not too thickly but evenly. Now spread a little bit of the wasabi on top. Attention! The stuff is sharp. Then spread the shrimp approximately in the middle and parallel to the lower margin of the nori. Add strips of spring onion and carrot in the middle as required.

4. Moisten the exposed edge and wrap a roll using a kitchen towel. Press firmly ... Done! .... Cut the roll into slices in the refrigerator and shortly before serving.

5. A bowl of soy sauce and the pickled ginger are served.

6. Do the same for the crab meat and salmon.

THIN SUSHI ROLLS

INGREDIENTS FOR 1 PORTIONS

- 500 g of rice, finished sushi
- 1 can of wasabi paste
- 1 point of nori sheets

For the filling:

- Cucumber
- Carrot
- 200 g of salmon fillet, skinned
- 200 g of fish fillet, (tuna fillet)
- Radish, japanese, pickled
- Avocado
- 2 tbsp of rice vinegar
- 250 ml of water
- Soy sauce
- Pickled ginger

PREPARATION

Total time approx. 30 minutes

1. Depending on your taste, choose the filling and cut the vegetables into chopsticks approx. 1 cm thick and the fish into pieces as thick as pencils.

2. Mix rice vinegar and water in a small bowl.

3. Place a bamboo mat on the work surface. Fold a nori sheet in half and break apart. Place the glossy, smooth side of the nori sheet half down on the bamboo mat.

4. Dip your hands in the vinegar water so that the rice does not stick to it. Take a handful of rice and form an elongated block.

5. Place the rice in the middle of the nori sheet and spread it evenly with your fingertips. Leave a 1 cm wide strip at the top.

6. Brush the rice in the middle with a little wasabi paste, do not overdo it, the wasabi taste should not overlap that of the ingredients.

7. Place a strip of fish or vegetables on the wasabi-coated rice. Raise the front end of the bamboo mat and slowly roll it up.

8. Roll up so far that the end of the nori sheet meets the edge of the rice. Apply light pressure to shape the roll.

9. Now only the free Nori strip looks out. Carefully shape the roll with both hands. Set the sushi roll aside and form the remaining rolls.

10. Dip a paper towel in the vinegar water and use it to wipe a sharp knife with a damp cloth. Halve the rolls with the knife.

11. Moisten the blade with the cloth after each cut. Place both roll halves in a row and cut twice so that 6 pieces of the same size are made. Arrange on a plate and serve with soy sauce and pickled ginger.

THICK SUSHI ROLLS

INGREDIENTS FOR 1 PORTIONS

- 500 g of rice, finished sushi
- 1 pack of nori sheets
- Wasabi paste

For the filling:

- Carrot cut into thin strips
- Cucumber, cut into thin strips
- 200 g of salmon or tuna cut into pencil-sized chopsticks
- Radish, japanese, pickled
- 1 pack of beans, green, cut into small pieces and steamed
- Avocado, cut into thin strips
- Tofu bags cut into 1 cm thick strips
- 2 tbsp of rice vinegar
- 250 ml of water
- Soy sauce
- Pickled ginger

PREPARATION

Total time approx. 45 minutes

1. Depending on your taste, choose the filling and cut the vegetables into chopsticks approx. 1 cm thick and the fish into pieces as thick as pencils.

2. Mix rice vinegar and water in a small bowl. Place a bamboo mat on the work surface. Place a nori sheet on the bamboo mat with the glossy, smooth side down.

3. Dip your hands in the vinegar water so that the rice does not stick to it. Take a handful of rice and form an elongated block.

4. Place 2 blocks of rice in the middle of the nori sheet and spread them evenly with your fingertips. Leave a 4 cm wide strip free at the top. Brush the rice in the middle with a little wasabi paste, do not overdo it, the wasabi taste should not overlap that of the ingredients.

5. Place a strip of fish on the wasabi-coated rice. Frame with vegetable strips on both sides. Raise the front end of the bamboo mat and slowly roll it up. Hold the filling with your middle, ring and little finger in place.

6. Roll up so far that the end of the nori sheet meets the edge of the rice. Apply light pressure to shape the roll.

7. Now only the Free Nori Strip looks out. Carefully shape the roll with both hands. Set the sushi roll aside and form the remaining rolls.

8. Dip a tea towel in the vinegar water and use it to wipe a sharp knife with a damp cloth. Halve the rolls with the knife.

9. Moisten the blade with the cloth after each cut. Place both roll halves in a row and cut twice so that 6 pieces of the same size are created. Arrange on a plate and serve with soy sauce and pickled ginger.

MUSHROOM SUSHI ROLLS

INGREDIENTS FOR 4 PORTIONS

- 3 cups of round grain rice
- 0.33 cups of rice vinegar
- 3 tbsp of sugar
- 1 teaspoon of salt, painted
- 8 shiitake mushrooms, dried, for the filling
- 0.33 cups of water (shiitake soaking water)
- 0.67 cups of dashi (1 pinch of instant fish broth dissolved in 0.66 cups of water)
- 1½ tbsp of sugar
- ½ tbsp of sake (japanese rice wine) or white wine
- 1 tbsp of soy sauce
- 1 egg
- 1 teaspoon of sugar
- 1 pinch salt
- Oil, for frying
- 100 g of spinach leaves
- Nori leaves (seaweed leaves)
- Soy sauce for dipping

PREPARATION

Total time approx. 1 hour 30 minutes

1. Boil the rice and put it in a bowl (ideally an untreated wooden bowl that can absorb excess water).

2. While the rice is cooking, stir the vinegar dressing (vinegar, sugar, salt) until the sugar has dissolved. It is best to warm up briefly.

3. Pour the vinegar dressing over the rice and mix well with a wooden spoon. Then let it cool down.

4. Soak the shiitake mushrooms in a bowl with lukewarm water for approx. 20 min. Drain and store the soaking water. Cut mushrooms into 7 - 8 mm wide strips.

5. Boil the mushrooms together with the ingredients water to soy sauce in a small saucepan and cook over low heat until the excess liquid has evaporated.

6. Beat the 3 eggs, whisk the sugar to salt with ingredients and strain through a tea strainer. Heat a little oil in a pan and bake a thick pancake from the entire (!) Dough. Let it cool and cut into strips about 1 cm long.

7. Blanch the spinach leaves, quench in cold water and wring out well.

8. Place Nori on a bamboo mat with the smooth side down. Spread about a quarter of the sushi rice evenly with wet hands. Leave about 1 cm of the Nori sheet free at the front.

9. Spread a quarter of the spinach, ice cream strips and mushrooms in the middle of the nori sheet.

10. Shape a firm roll using the bamboo mat. Then press them down with your fingers and shape them.

11. Do the same with the remaining ingredients. Cut each of the 4 sushi rolls into about 8 slices.

12. Dip in soy sauce before eating.

FISH AND CHIPS SUSHI ROLLS

INGREDIENTS FOR 4 PORTIONS

- 500 g of sushi rice or good milk rice
- 4 tbsp of powder (sushi vinegar powder "sushinoko")
- 8 fish fingers with white meat
- 200 g of french fries, frozen
- 4 nori sheets
- Mayonnaise
- Ketchup

PREPARATION

Total time approx. 50 minutes

1. Sushi vinegar powder is available in the Asian shop. Alternatively, the sushi rice can also be cooked with sushi vinegar, choosing a recipe from the database.

2. Pre-heat the oven to 220 degrees Celsius. Wash the rice 2 or 3 times in a saucepan, then drain the water. Put 700 ml of cold water in the saucepan and let the rice rest for 10 minutes. Please make sure that the pot holds more than 1.8 l and has a blanket!

3. Place baking paper on the baking sheet, spread the fries and fish sticks on top and slide the baking sheet into the oven. It takes about 20 minutes for fries and fish sticks to be ready.

4. Now cook the rice. To do this, place the saucepan on an electric stove at maximum setting (3) and wait until foam comes out of the saucepan. It takes about 10 to 15 minutes. Then turn the heat to zero and leave the pan on the stove for 15 minutes. Please note that the size of the pot may prevent the foam from coming out. To avoid stuck rice, check from time to time - but not often! - Whether there is still liquid. When the liquid has been used up, turn the heat to zero immediately and leave the pan on the stove for 15 minutes. When the rice is ready, put the rice in a bowl and mix in the sushi vinegar powder. This will make the rice smooth.

5. Take the fish fingers and fries out of the oven when they're done

6. Now the roll comes. There are several tips for this, but my recommendation is to wrap a bamboo mat with cling film so that the rice doesn't stick to the mat.

7. Place on the mat of nori leaves and spread the rice on top. Spread 2 fish sticks and French fries on the rice and add majo and ketchup on top. Shape everything into a roll using the bamboo mat.

BUCKWHEAT SUSHI ROLLS

INGREDIENTS FOR 2 PORTIONS

- 200 g of buckwheat
- Rice vinegar
- Sugar
- 1 teaspoon flour, dissolved in cold water
- Nori sheets
- 150 g of smoked salmon
- 400 g of mixed vegetables, e.g. Carrot, cucumber, avocado, bell pepper, asparagus, radish, ...
- 4 tbsp of soy sauce
- 2 tsp of wasabi powder
- 2 tsp of pickled ginger

PREPARATION

Total time approx. 1 hour 20 minutes

1. Boil the buckwheat in double the amount of water for 20 minutes. Salt the water if necessary. Then leave the buckwheat covered for 20 minutes and mix in some rice vinegar and sugar. Then add the flour or starch dissolved in water and heat again. Stir in the buckwheat. It should have a sticky consistency.

2. After it has cooled a little, spread the buckwheat as a thin layer on a nori sheet, which lies on a bamboo mat. The edges should be left a little free. Then place the desired contents, i.e. vegetables and fish, in the middle of the length of the coated sheet and roll it up using the bamboo mat and press firmly together. Knowledge of sushi and practice are almost essential here. Now cut the pieces down with a sharp knife wetted with vinegar. The edge pieces can be tried on this occasion.

3. Divide the soy sauce, the wasabi and the ginger into 2 portions, put them in separate bowls and serve with the buckwheat sushi. The soy sauce is used for short dipping, the wasabi for careful spreading and the ginger between the sushi pieces for "neutralizing", refreshing and snacking.

CRISPY BIG SUSHI ROLLS

INGREDIENTS FOR 2 PORTIONS

- Raw salmon
- Carrot
- Cucumber
- Avocado
- Philadelphia
- 5 Nori sheets
- Rice (sushi rice)
- Breadcrumbs
- Fat for the pan

PREPARATION

Total time approx. 45 minutes

1. Cook the sushi rice as usual (possibly take a recipe from the database). Peel the carrots and cut lengthways into quarters. Cut the cucumber into 1 - 1 1/2 cm strips. Let the carrot and cucumber strips cool in the pan with a little water, briefly steam the sugar and salt. Cut the salmon lengthways into strips as well as the avocado.

2. Now cover the nori sheet with sushi rice. Place the ingredients for the filling in the first third and spread some of the cream cheese lengthways (preferably along the salmon). Now brush the not yet cut sushi roll with a little whisked egg white and roll through the breadcrumbs. Fry immediately in the hot pan with a little (!) Fat (not too long, so that the fish doesn't cook, it's really very quick)

3. Dab on kitchen paper and cut into slices. With soy sauce, pickled ginger and Thai chili sauce it tastes particularly good! The recipe can also be supplemented with surimi and pickled mustard cabbage.

CAULIFLOWER SUSHI ROLLS

INGREDIENTS FOR 3 PORTIONS

- 700 g of cauliflower,
- 150 ml of water, cold
- 1 g of guar gum
- 2 tbsp of rice vinegar
- Sweetener of your choice (e.g. 1 tbsp sukrin)
- Salt
- 5 nori sheets

For the filling:

- Shrimp and / or avocado, salmon, cucumber
- Wasabi paste

PREPARATION

Total time approx. 40 minutes

1. Wash the cauliflower and cut it into pieces, grate it in the food processor and boil it with about ¼ l water for 5-10 minutes. Drain and squeeze through a clean tea towel. Mix 1 g guar gum with 150 ml cold water. Put the cauliflower back in the pot or in a bowl and mix well with the sukrin, rice vinegar, salt and guar water mix until a thick porridge has formed.

2. Place the nori sheets on the sushi mat, spread the cauliflower porridge about ½ cm thick and then topping with z. Shrimp, avocado, salmon and cucumber, brush with a little wasabi paste and then roll in, press well, leave something to stand and then cut into pieces with a damp, sharp knife.

EGG SUSHI ROLLS

INGREDIENTS FOR 2 PORTIONS

- 1 big egg
- Seasoned salt
- Salt and pepper
- 2 teaspoons of cream cheese
- 3 discs of smoked salmon, or other fish, whether or not raw
- 3 sheets of nori sheets
- Vegetables, e.g. Avocado, cucumber, carrots
- Soy sauce
- Wasabi paste
- Ginger root, inlaid

PREPARATION

Total time approx. 35 minutes

1. Mix egg white, egg, pepper, salt, fry on both sides and halve to an omelet.

2. Cut the vegetables and salmon into thin strips.

3. Spread the nori sheets on a mat or baking paper and top with half of the omelette. Maybe the leaves still need to be cut. Brush the omelette with the cream cheese and top with vegetables and fish. Brush the ends of the leaves with water.

4. Roll the nori sheets tightly from one side to the other. Then cut the roll into two centimeters pieces, serve with soy sauce, wasabi and the pickled ginger.

VEGAN SUSHI ROLLS

INGREDIENTS FOR 4 PORTIONS

- 300 g of sushi rice
- 600 ml of water
- 60 ml of rice vinegar
- 1 teaspoon of sugar
- ½ tsp of salt
- 5 Nori sheets
- 1 small salad cucumber, cut into strips
- 1 tomato cut into strips
- 1 small avocado cut into strips

Furthermore:

- Soy sauce
- Wasabi

PREPARATION

Total time approx. 50 minutes

1. Wash the sushi rice in a colander under cold running water until the water runs clear.

2. Then drain the sushi rice well.

3. Bring 600 ml of water to a boil in a saucepan, add the rice and reduce the heat, put the lid on and let it boil for 10 minutes. Remove the rice from the heat and cover with a dry, clean tea towel and let it evaporate for 10 to 15 minutes. Meanwhile heat the rice vinegar, dissolve the salt and sugar in it.

4. Put the rice in a bowl and add the rice vinegar and mix regularly with a wooden spatula and let cool.

5. Place a nori sheet on a sushi mat, spread 1 cm of rice on top, leaving a strip at the top. Place the cleaned and cut vegetables in the middle. Roll up the nori sheet evenly, then gently press the sushi into the bamboo mat until it has a slightly rectangular shape. This takes practice.

6. Cut the sushi into slice-wide slices with a sharp knife and serve with soy sauce and wasabi.

7. Other seasonal raw vegetables can also be used for the filling.

VEGAN SUSHI DELUXE

INGREDIENTS FOR 2 PORTIONS

- ½ cup of sushi rice
- 2 tbsp of rice vinegar (rice wine vinegar)
- ½ avocado
- ½ red pepper
- ½ carrot
- ¼ cucumber
- 4 nori sheets

Sausages, vegan (Merguez sausages)

- Wasabi paste
- Soy sauce

PREPARATION

Total time approx. 50 minutes

1. Put on the rice with twice the amount of water, bring to the boil briefly and then let it swell on a low flame for 15 minutes. Then remove from the heat, stir in the rice vinegar and let it cool down, otherwise the nori sheets will soak.

2. Cut the avocado, bell pepper, carrot, cucumber and the sausage lengthways into thin chopsticks. Core the cucumber with a teaspoon before cutting.

3. Place a nori sheet on the bamboo mat and cover the lower third with rice. Spread a strip of wasabi paste, the vegetable sticks and the merguez on top. Roll up firmly using the bamboo mat and cut the roll into several pieces using a damp, clean knife. Do the same with the other nori sheets.

4. Serve the sushi with a bowl of soy sauce.

VEGAN SPICY SUSHI ROLLS

INGREDIENTS FOR 2 PORTIONS

- 4 nori sheets
- Chorizo, vegan
- ½ cup of sushi rice
- ½ bell pepper, red
- ½ avocado
- Salt
- Soy sauce

Also: (for the chipotle mayonnaise)

- 2 teaspoons of sauce (adobo sauce)
- Jalapeños (chipotle in adobo sauce)
- 50 ml of mayonnaise, vegan

PREPARATION

Total time approx. 30 minutes

1. Cut the avocado, bell peppers and the sausage lengthways into thin strips. Place the rice with twice the amount of water and a pinch of salt, bring to the boil briefly and then let it swell on a low flame for 15 minutes until the water is completely boiled. Afterwards, let it cool down, otherwise the nori sheets will soak.

2. Place a nori sheet on the bamboo mat and cover the lower third with rice. Spread 2 teaspoons of chipotle mayonnaise on the rice. Then spread a row of vegetable sticks and chorizo on each. Roll up firmly using the bamboo mat and cut the roll into several pieces using a damp, clean knife. Do the same with the other nori sheets.

3. Serve the sushi with a bowl of soy sauce.

VEGETABLE SUSHI ROLLS

INGREDIENTS FOR 1 PORTIONS

- 70 g of sushi rice
- Salt
- 15 ml of rice vinegar
- 5 g of sugar
- 2 nori sheets
- 100 g of peas, frozen, or beans, white, cooked
- 50 g of soy quark (quark alternative)
- ½ tsp of wasabi powder
- 15 ml of soy sauce
- 1 small piece of ginger, fresher
- Garlic cloves
- Salt
- 1 pinch cayenne pepper
- 1½ of carrot, alternatively kohlrabi, beetroot, cucumber, peppers grated or cut into thin sticks,
- Spring onions
- Soy sauce
- Ginger

PREPARATION

Total time approx. 50 minutes

1. Place the sushi rice in a sieve and rinse thoroughly with water. Then the sushi rice in salted water with the lid closed over low heat for about 15 minutes. Simmer. Switch off the stove and the rice for another 5 min. let swell. Remove the lid, stir in the rice vinegar and sugar and let the sushi rice cool completely.

2. In the meantime, puree the peas / beans with soy curd, wasabi powder, soy sauce, ginger and garlic to a creamy mass. Possibly. Season with salt and cayenne pepper.

3. When the sushi rice has cooled completely, mix about 2/3 of the cream with the sushi rice.

4. Wash, peel and prepare the vegetables ready for cooking (cut into thin strips, grate, etc.).

5. Place the two nori sheets on the sushi mat with the rough side upwards with about 2 cm overlap. Spread the rice evenly over half of it evenly on the nori sheet. Top with the vegetables and the rest of the cream and use the sushi mat to gently roll them in with light pressure. At the end, leave about 2 cm of Nori sheet, moisten with water and seal the XXL roll.

VEGETABLE SUSHI MIX

INGREDIENTS FOR 1 PORTIONS

- 1 cup of rice (sushi or basmati rice)
- Water
- ½ carrot
- ¼ bell pepper, red
- Cucumber
- 1 teaspoon of wasabi powder or paste
- 1 shot of sake or dry white wine
- Rice vinegar
- 1 teaspoon of sugar
- Soy sauce, japanese
- Sesame oil or sunflower oil

PREPARATION

Total time approx. 15 minutes

1. First put the rice on according to the package instructions and let it simmer until there is no more water in the pot. In the meantime, wash the vegetables, peel the carrot and cucumber and cut everything into small, visually appealing pieces (diamonds, cubes, chopsticks ...).

2. Heat the oil in a pan and add the carrots first, then the peppers and finally the cucumber and cook until firm. Then deglaze the whole thing with a little rice vinegar, sake and a dash of soy sauce (not too much of the soy sauce, otherwise the vegetables will turn brown). Sprinkle the sugar over it and let the liquid reduce.

3. Now put the finished rice on a plate and spread the vegetables over it. Finally, mix wasabi with soy sauce (amount depending on taste) and drizzle over the dish.

CHEESE SUSHI ROLLS

INGREDIENTS FOR 2 PORTIONS

- 200 g of feta cheese
- 350 g of cream cheese, grainy
- ½ cucumber
- 150 g of smoked salmon
- 5 nori sheets
- Soy sauce, to taste

PREPARATION

Total time approx. 35 minutes

1. Crumble the feta cheese and mix it carefully with the granular cream cheese. Cut the smoked salmon into strips. Peel the cucumber, scrape out the kernels inside with a spoon and cut the meat into long strips.
2. Place the nori sheet on the mat and brush 2/3 with the cheese paste (not too thick), put on a strip of smoked salmon and cucumber and roll it up like normal sushi. Let it rest a little so that the nori sheets can wet out, then cut into rolls about 3-4 cm long. Serve with soy sauce.

TOFU SUSHI ROLLS

INGREDIENTS FOR 5 PORTIONS

- 200 g of tofu, seasoned
- 200 g of arborio rice
- 100 g of bamboo shoot, inlaid
- 400 ml of water
- 200 ml of rice vinegar
- 10 pieces of nori sheets
- 4 tbsp of soy sauce
- 4 tbsp of oil (sunflower)

PREPARATION

Total time approx. 30 minutes

1. Cut the tofu into elongated slices and fry in a pan with oil and soy sauce. Let cool down. Then briefly heat the seasoned tofu in the same pan.
2. Simmer the rice with the water until the water is absorbed (approx. 15 min.).
3. Spread the rice on the algae so that about 3/4 of the leaf is covered. Put in tofu and bamboo shoots. Roll up the algae leaves using a mat or a kitchen towel. Brush the last quarter with rice vinegar and glue the roll tightly with it.
4. Cut each roll into 5 pieces.

AVOCADO SUSHI ROLLS

INGREDIENTS FOR 2 PORTIONS

- 100 g of sushi rice
- 4 nori sheets
- 5 tbsp of rice vinegar
- 2 tbsp of sugar
- Salt
- Avocado

PREPARATION

Total time approx. 55 minutes

1. You also need a makisu (bamboo mat) to make sushi.

2. First, the sushi rice is washed thoroughly until the water is clear. Then it is boiled in cold water, over medium heat for 15 min. long.

3. In the meantime you can mix and heat the rice vinegar with sugar and salt. When the rice is cooked, add the vinegar, stir and cover with a cotton cloth and 10 min. to let go.

4. Then wrap the bamboo mat with cling film and cut a nori sheet in half.

5. Halve an avocado, remove the peel and cut into slightly thicker slices.

6. Now spread the cooled rice on the nori sheet, leaving 1 cm free at the top and moistening this strip with water. Place the avocado in the middle and roll everything carefully with a little pressure. Finally, cut the roll into bite-size pieces.

7. Serve with wasabi, pickled ginger and soy sauce.

SHIITAKE MUSHROOMS FOR SUSHI ROLLS

INGREDIENTS FOR 2 PORTIONS

- 10 shiitake mushrooms, dried
- 2 tbsp of soy sauce
- 2 tbsp of sugar
- 2 teaspoons of mirin

PREPARATION

Total time approx. 30 minutes

1. The shiitake mushrooms are ideal for vegetarian sushi, e.g. shiitake cream cheese maki.

2. Cover the dried shiitake mushrooms with boiling water and soak them for 15 minutes. Alternatively, you can also take cold water and soak it for an hour (this will make the mushroom aroma even more intense).

3. Drain the mushrooms and collect the soaking water. If necessary, remove the hard stem ends. If the mushrooms are used for sushi, it is advisable to cut them into strips at this point.

4. Cover the mushrooms in a saucepan with the soaking water and bring to a boil, then reduce the heat and simmer for 2 minutes. Add the sugar and soy sauce and simmer, stirring occasionally, until the liquid has completely evaporated.

5. Finally add the mirin and stir. The last step is not absolutely necessary, but the mirin gives the mushrooms the finishing touch.

SHIITAKE SUSHI ROLLS

INGREDIENTS FOR 4 PORTIONS

- 4 mushrooms (shiitake), dried
- 2 tbsp of soy sauce, japanese
- 1 tbsp of sugar

PREPARATION

Total time approx. 40 minutes

1. Soak mushrooms in hot water for about 20 minutes. Remove the stems and cut the heads into fine strips. Simmer in 1/2 cup of the soaking liquid together with the soy sauce and sugar until the liquid has almost evaporated. Let cool down.

2. Work the mushroom strips into maki sushi (rice inner rolls). They look very good in color (brown) as well as aromatic (sweet, umami, and sour) and form a nice contrast to vegetable strips.

CAPRESE SUSHI ROLLS

INGREDIENTS FOR 1 PORTIONS

- 2 nori sheets
- 1 port of rice (sushi rice), ready prepared, recipes in the database
- 1 ball of mozzarella
- Tomatoes
- Basil

PREPARATION

Total time approx. 20 minutes

1. Halve the nori sheet lengthways. Place one half on the bamboo mat and cover with rice. Cut the mozzarella into small pencils. Wash the tomatoes and also cut them into sticks, first cut them into slices, cut out the inside and make the sticks out of the firm rim of the tomato. Wash the basil. Spread the tomato and mozzarella sticks on the rice, and the basil leaves as well. Form everything into a roll.

2. Do the same with the second half of the nori sheet.

HERBAL MUSHROOM SUSHI ROLLS

INGREDIENTS FOR 2 PORTIONS

- 300 g of herbal mushrooms
- 180 g of shirati rice noodles
- 2 tbsp of cream cheese
- 200 g of pak choi
- Spring onion
- Coriander
- 4 nori sheets

PREPARATION

Total time approx. 40 minutes

1. Slice the herb mushrooms lengthways and fry them in the pan with a little butter or oil. You can be a little tanned for the aroma. Let cool down.

2. Cut the pak choi, if necessary cut the leaves lengthways and briefly fry in the pan over high heat. It should remain crisp.

3. Clean the green from the spring onions and cut into strips.

4. Wash the shirataki in a colander. If they smell fishy (due to the alkaline liquid), rinse them briefly with vinegar, then rinse the vinegar as well. Drain well and then mix with the cream cheese.

5. Spread a third of each on a nori sheet, place 1/3 spring onions, 1/3 mushrooms and 1/3 pak choi lengthways on top. If you like coriander, you can sprinkle chopped coriander over it. Roll up and cut into slices.

6. Serve with soy sauce and wasabi.

CARROT AND CUCUMBER SUSHI ROLLS

INGREDIENTS FOR 4 PORTIONS

- 500 g of rice pudding
- 5 tbsp of rice vinegar or brandy vinegar
- 4 carrots
- Cucumber
- 8 nori sheets
- Olive oil

PREPARATION

Total time approx. 1 hour

1. We thought about the variant with the milk rice, because we could not buy sushi rice. We think it tastes delicious too!

2. Place the rice in the rice cooker and wash twice thoroughly with lukewarm water. Drain the water and smooth the rice a little. Then spread 2-3 tablespoons of rice vinegar on the rice. Pour the cooking water up to 2-3 finger-widths above the rice surface and cook the rice. When the rice cooker has switched off, leave the sushi rice covered for another 10 minutes. Then switch off the rice cooker completely and let the rice cool down. For this purpose, the lid can also be opened.

3. The rice can also be prepared the evening before (if there is to be sushi for lunch). However, do not open the lid overnight, just switch off the cooker and let the rice cool down, otherwise the surface will become very dry and part of the rice will then no longer be usable.

4. Wash, peel and quarter the carrots for the carrot sushi. Fry in a hot pan in plenty of olive oil for about 5 minutes, remove and place on a plate! Place the bamboo mat on a smooth surface and place a nori sheet on it. Then spread rice with a dough scraper approx. 3-5 mm thick over the entire surface of the leaf. Now place 2-3 slices of carrot 2 cm from the edge and form a roll. Depending on how thick you want the sushi to be later, the filling must be measured. A little feeling is required! Now cut the sushi roll into approx. 3 cm thick slices and arrange on a platter. 4 nori sheets are used for the carrot sushi, the other half for the cucumber sushi.

5. Wash, peel the cucumber (possibly leave some peel), quarter lengthways and core. Then cut it again across the length of the nori sheet. Simmer the cucumber slices in a brew of water and 2 tablespoons of vinegar for about 5 minutes, also remove and place on a plate. Proceed as for the carrot sushi.

SUSHI WITH CAULIFLOWER

INGREDIENTS FOR 2 PORTIONS

- 1 gr of head cauliflower
- Salt
- 30 ml of rice vinegar
- 20 g of sugar (1 tbsp.)
- 1 teaspoon of oyster sauce
- 100 g of double cream cheese
- 100 g of salmon
- Cucumber
- Vegetables or fish of your choice
- 4 nori sheets
- Soy sauce
- Wasabi

PREPARATION

Total time approx. 2 hours 44 minutes

1. Divide the cauliflower into florets and wash. Bring lightly salted water to a boil. Put the cauliflower in the boiling water and cook for 4 minutes, it should remain very firm to the bite. Drain well and let cool. Granulate with the food processor or blender.

2. Mix the vinegar with the sugar and the oyster sauce and heat briefly so that everything combines well. Then pour over the cauliflower and mix with the cream cheese to a mass.

3. Cut vegetables and fish into thin strips.

4. Maki:

5. Spread a cauliflower mass on a nori sheet. Leave the upper edge approx. 2 cm free. Spread a little wasabi on it if you like. Place the vegetable and fish strips lengthways in the middle. Moisten the edge with water so that it sticks better together. Now wrap it into a tight roll with a sushi mat. Chill the roll for an hour, then cut into pieces of equal size.

6. Nigiri:

7. Form small blocks by hand or with a nigiri form from the cauliflower mass. Brush with wasabi and top with fish. Chill for an hour too.

CALIFORNIA ROLLS

INGREDIENTS FOR 1 PORTIONS

- 500 g of rice, sushi finished
- 1 pack of nori sheets
- Mayonnaise
- Wasabi paste
- 2 tbsp of rice vinegar
- 250 ml of water

For the filling:

- 1 pack of surimi
- Avocado, cut into thin strips
- Salad cucumber, cut into thin strips
- 50 g of roe from the fly fish
- Sesame, black and white
- Soy sauce
- Pickled ginger

PREPARATION

Total time approx. 45 minutes

1. Mix rice vinegar and water in a small bowl.

2. Place a bamboo mat on the work surface and wrap in cling film. Fold a nori sheet in half and break apart. Place the halved nori sheet on the mat.

3. Dip your hands in the vinegar water so that the rice does not stick to it. Take a handful of rice and form an elongated block.

4. Place the rice in the middle of the nori sheet and spread it evenly with your fingertips. Lift the rice-covered nori leaf and turn it over quickly.

5. Place the imitation crab meat and the cucumber strips in the middle of the nori sheet, pull a narrow strip of mayonnaise, seasoned with wasabi, and place the avocado strips on top.

6. Lift the bamboo mat and hold the filling if necessary. Start rolling up. Squeeze the roll lightly and give it a rectangular shape with gentle pressure.

7. Roll the mat apart again. Spread the fries on the sushi roll and press gently with a spoon. Turn the roll over to cover the underside with roe.

8. Dip a tea towel in the vinegar water and use it to wipe a sharp knife with a damp cloth. Halve the rolls with the knife.

9. Moisten the blade with the cloth after each cut. Place both roll halves in a row and cut twice so that 6 pieces of the same size are made. Arrange on a plate and serve with soy sauce and pickled ginger.

CALIFORNIA ROLLS - SALMON AND AVOCADO

INGREDIENTS FOR 1 PORTIONS

- Avocado
- Nori sheets
- 350 g of rice (sushi), cooked
- 100 g of cream cheese
- 300 g of salmon fillet, very fresh
- Wasabi paste
- Ginger root, pickled
- Soy sauce

PREPARATION

Total time approx. 30 minutes

1. Peel the avocado, remove the core, cut into 12 strips about 7 cm long. Halve the algae leaves. Cover a bamboo mat with cling film. Approx. spread 120 g of rice on top, press well. Place 1/2 seaweed leaf on top, spread with 25 g cream cheese, spread 3 avocado strips on each. Roll up and press together using the mat. Take out the sushi. Cut salmon into thin, large (approx. 5 x 22 cm) pieces and wrap them around the sushi roll. Cut into 8 pieces. Process the remaining ingredients in the same way. Serve sushi with wasabi, ginger and soy sauce.

2. Basic sushi rice recipe for approx. 500 g of cooked rice:

3. Wash 350 g sushi rice (e.g. American short grain rice) until the water remains clear. Approx. Soak in cold water for 30 minutes and drain. Place in a saucepan with 500 ml of water and possibly 1 piece of seaweed and cook over a medium heat for about 15 minutes. Remove the kelp, pull the pot off the stove and let it swell for about 15 minutes. Mix in 3 tablespoons of rice vinegar, 2 tablespoons of sugar and salt with a wooden spoon while allowing the rice to cool.

CALIFORNIA ROLLS INSIDE OUT

INGREDIENTS FOR 12 PORTIONS

- 250 g of rice, sushi rice, ready made
- 5 nori sheets
- 40 g of surimi
- Salad cucumber, 2 strips, cut lengthways
- ½ avocado
- 1 teaspoon of lemon juice
- 4 tbsp of sesame
- 1 tbsp of horseradish (cream)

PREPARATION

Total time approx. 20 minutes

1. Roast the sesame seeds in a pan without fat until golden, let them cool on a flat plate. Pat the surimi sticks dry and cut in half lengthways. Wash the cucumber, cut in half lengthways and remove the seeds with a spoon, cut the length of 2 strips about 0.5 cm wide. Peel the avocado, cut lengthways into strips and immediately drizzle with lemon juice.

2. Wrap the sushi mat completely with cling film. Place a nori sheet with the smooth side down on top and cover completely with half of the rice. Press the rice lightly and then turn it over with the nori sheet so that the rice lies on the transparent film.

3. Spread half of the horseradish on the lower third of the nori sheet, spread half of the surimi sticks, cucumber sticks and avocados on each, and roll up the whole thing.

4. Form a second roll from the remaining ingredients. Cut the rolls into 6 pieces and roll each piece in toasted sesame.

CALIFORNIA SUSHI WRAPS

INGREDIENTS FOR 4 PORTIONS

- 250 g of Rice (sushi rice)
- ½ tsp of salt
- 2 tbsp of Rice vinegar
- 1 bunch of Spring onions
- 4 Tortillas (wheat tortillas)
- 4 Nori sheets
- 2 Carrots
- 1 Cucumber
- 1 bag of Surimi sticks (8 sticks)
- Soy sauce

PREPARATION

Total time approx. 1 day 30 minutes

1. Cook the sushi rice according to the package instructions. Meanwhile, cut the spring onions into thin rings. Grate the carrots finely, peel, quarter and core the cucumber. Then mix the rice with salt, rice vinegar and spring onions and let cool.

2. For each wrap, heat a tortilla in the microwave for 10 seconds. Place a nori sheet on the tortilla and spread 1/4 of the rice on top. Spread a thin layer of grated carrots on the rice. Place 1/4 of the cucumber and 2 surimis sticks on the edge of the wraps and start rolling up the wrap at this end. Wrap the ends about halfway through.

3. Wrap each wrap very tightly with cling film and put in the fridge for 24 hours. Cut the wraps diagonally in the middle and serve with soy sauce.

SUSHI MIX 1

INGREDIENTS FOR 4 PORTIONS

- 450 g of rice (sushi rice)
- 1 avocado
- 1 cucumber
- 1 tbsp of mayonnaise
- 2 tbsp of sesame seeds, toasted
- 150 g of salmon
- 1 pack of surimi (crab meat imitation)
- 6 shrimps
- 150 g of tuna
- Wasabi paste (spicy japanese horseradish paste)
- Nori leaves (algae leaves)
- Pickled ginger (gari)
- Soy sauce
- Salad leaves, e.g. Lollo rosso

PREPARATION

Total time approx. 45 minutes

Before you start, wrap the sushi mat with cling film, so the mat stays clean and the rice cannot stick in the spaces between the thin bamboo sticks.

Maki with salmon

Take a nori sheet and cut it in half with a knife. Place the sheet on the bamboo mat with the rough side up so that the rice adheres better. Now lightly dampen the fingers in a bowl with water and spread a lot of cooled rice on the nori sheet so that the algae leaf is covered with rice, only a free edge should remain at the bottom so that the roll can be glued later. Now cut the salmon in stick form and place them lengthwise on the rice. Brush the salmon with wasabi, but only thinly, because wasabi is quite hot. Then moisten the uncovered edge of the nori sheet and, starting from the other side, fold in the bamboo mat so that a roll is created. If you press the rolled-up bamboo mat from above and from the sides, you get a square shape.

California Roll or Inside-Out

Take half a sheet of algae, place it on the front area of the mat and cover the rough side completely with rice, sprinkle sesame on the rice. Take the free side of the bamboo mat, fold over the algae leaf with the rice, press and turn, so we now have the other side of the algae leaf in front of us, the rice is below. Spread a little mayonnaise lengthways on the algae leaf, add the surimi lengthways to the mayo, cut the cucumber and avocado into sticks and add. Brush with a little wasabi and finally put a little Lollo Rosso on top. Now roll the whole thing in with the help of the bamboo mat.

Nigiris with tuna and shrimps

To do this, cut the tuna into bite-sized thin slices, free shrimp from their shell. Brush both with a little wasabi. Moisten the hands, take some rice and roll it oval in the back of the hand and then press it into a box shape. Place the fish on the rice.

The number of nigiris in relation to the makis depends on your preferences, if you prefer makis, just make more sushi rolls. Here, a roll can of course also become completely vegetarian, for example with only avocado or shiitake mushrooms or with your own taste also varied with vegetables and fish. Of course, you can also use other sea creatures for the Nigiris, such as salmon, octopus, mackerel, scallop, etc. Just think in advance when shopping to adjust the amount of sea ingredients to your requirements. And make sure you always buy fresh fish, the best thing to say is that you want to make sushi.

For serving, cut the rolls into approx. 6 to 8 pieces, take a sharp knife and moisten them slightly before each cut, so you have clean cuts and no rice sticking anywhere on the edges of the roll. Arrange the pieces with the nigiris on a plate. Serve the pickled ginger and soy sauce in separate bowls. Both nigiris and makis can be dipped in the soy sauce, which gives additional taste, and the wasabi paste can also be added. The ginger is used to neutralize the taste between two different sushi snacks, but some also simply eat it.

Have fun rolling and enjoy your meal!

SUSHI MIX 2

INGREDIENTS FOR 6 PORTIONS

- 4 nori sheets
- 2 cups of rice (sushi rice)
- 3 tbsp of rice vinegar
- 1 tbsp of sugar
- 1 teaspoon of salt
- 2 tbsp of wasabi paste or 2 tbsp. Wasabi powder, mixed with water
- 2 tbsp of mayonnaise
- 1 teaspoon of spice mix (togarashi)
- 100 g of salmon (sushi quality)
- 100 g of tuna (sushi quality)
- Surimi
- ½ cucumber, peeled, seeded
- Avocado, seeded, without skin
- 6 large shrimps, raw, without head
- 1 disc of ginger, very thin, grated
- Salt

- 1 tbsp of sesame oil
- 2 tbsp of sesame, black
- 2 tbsp of caviar (tobiko - fly fish caviar)
- 6 discs of pancakes (japanese omelet)
- 2 teaspoons of caviar (trout caviar)
- 1 tbsp of cress
- 2 tbsp of ginger (gari - sushi ginger) from the glass or homemade
- 20 ml of soy sauce

PREPARATION

Total time approx. 45 minutes

1. Sushi means using leavened rice. Raw fish does not have to be part of it. First, the vinegar is warmed up and mixed well with the sugar and salt. This process should take place days in advance because the longer the mixture is at rest, the better it gets. 4 weeks would be optimal and the mixture does not have to be refrigerated. Once the rice is acidified, it only lasts about a day.

2. The rice is washed until only clear water flows out. Then let it drain in the sieve for 30 minutes. It will work perfectly in a rice cooker with a pinch of salt. If you don't have a cooker, you can read the exact instructions in the database under my recipe "Japanese rice".

3. When the rice is ready, put it in a baking dish (not made of metal) and distribute it well. It would be better to use a Japanese wooden mold that is specially designed for sushi rice. Then pour the vinegar mixture over the rice and work it into it with a wooden spatula. Do not stir, but prick and turn horizontally to distribute the vinegar well.

4. To prevent it from cooling completely, so that the rice doesn't stick too much, cover it with a slightly damp cloth. If the rice is needed, it should only be at room temperature so that the contents are not cooked.

5. At the latest now all ingredients should be portioned. Cut two cucumbers, a salmon and tuna strand about 0.5 cm thick and a length the width of the nori sheet. Stone the avocado, remove the peel and trim on strands of equal thickness. These must then be put together later.

6. Take the prawns out of their shells, remove the intestines and insert a toothpick lengthways so that they stay perfectly in shape. Now cook gently in the sesame oil, mix in the ginger and lightly salt, add a little Togarashi, set aside to cool.

7. For maki sushi, the nori sheet is cut in half and one, with the rough side up, is placed on the lower half of a sushi bast mat. Now spread the rice about 0.5 cm thick with wet hands and press it on, while 1 - 2 cm remain free on the nori sheet. In the middle you put a cucumber strand and next to it a tuna strand, which you spread thinly with wasabi.

8. Now roll up the nori sheet using the bast mat, pressing everything together relatively firmly. If necessary, moisten the vacant area on the nori sheet and close the roll there. Unroll the raffia mat again.

9. First halve the maki roll and then cut it into 6 parts. The knife for this must be of very good quality and should be rinsed with warm water after each cut. Use the other half of the nori sheet to make another roll with avocado and salmon.

SUSHI MIX 3

INGREDIENTS FOR 6 PORTIONS

- 1 kg of sushi rice
- 10 nori sheets
- 200 g of salmon, fresh
- 100 g of shrimp
- ½ cucumber, about length of nori sheets
- ½ avocado
- Carrot, about the length of the nori leaves
- Sesame
- Mirin
- Soy sauce
- Wasabi powder
- Ginger pickled
- 4 tbsp of sugar

Also: (for the japanese omelet)

- Egg
- 1 teaspoon of soy sauce
- 2 teaspoons of mirin
- Sugar

PREPARATION

Total time approx. 3 hours

1. First cook the sushi rice according to the package description. Meanwhile, heat 12 tablespoons of mirin with the sugar in a saucepan until the sugar has dissolved. Then pour the Mirin-Sud onto the finished sushi rice and fold in. Let the rice cool down.

2. Cut the cucumber, carrots and avocado into thin strips, adapting them to the length of the nori sheets. Do the same with some of the salmon, cut the other half into wider, short but thin pieces, which are later added to the nigiri. Cut the shrimp either lengthways so that they are flat on the nigiris or leave them untrimmed.

3. Wrap the bamboo mat with cling film so that no rice sticks in between and put a nori sheet on top. I cut away a third of each nori sheet and use this smaller part for the inside-out rolls, so the maki have a nice size. When the rice has cooled, spread a layer of rice on one of the nori sheets and make sure that the layer is not too thick. Now place either strips of fish, cucumber, carrot or avocado at the beginning of the roll and roll the roll with light pressure using the sushi mat.Put sesame seeds on a larger plate. For the inside-out rolls, put rice directly on the mat covered with cling film. Place the smaller part of the norbi leaf on top and fill again with strips of vegetables or fish. Now roll with the mat and turn the finished roll in sesame.

4. Form small amounts of rice for the nigiri and top with the salmon and prawns. You can also top it with omelette. For the Japanese omelet, I whisked 2 eggs, 1 teaspoon of soy sauce and 2 teaspoons of mirin with a little sugar and let them stand in the pan over low heat. Then cut into thin, wide slices, which can then be placed on the nigiri. I cut thin strips from a nori sheet here, wrap them in the middle around the nigiri and moisten them a little with a mixture of water and mirin.

5. Cut the sushi rolls into bite-size pieces and arrange them on serving plates with the nigiri. Mix wasabi powder with water or use ready paste. Place the soy sauce in shallow bowls and arrange the pickled ginger.

SUSHI BURRITO WITH TURKEY, MANGO AND AVOCADO

INGREDIENTS FOR 2 PORTIONS

- 200 g of sushi rice
- 2 tbsp of rice vinegar
- Sugar
- 200 g of turkey breast
- Cucumber
- Mango, ripe
- Avocado, ripe
- Arugula
- 3 tbsp of peanuts, salted
- 100 g of crème fraiche cheese
- 100 g of cream cheese
- Lemons
- 2 tbsp of oil, neutral
- Chili flakes
- Salt and pepper
- 4 nori sheets
- Soy sauce

PREPARATION

Total time approx. 1 hour 10 minutes

1. So that the sushi rice has cooled down to roll, you should prepare it first. First wash the sushi rice thoroughly. Then prepare the rice according to the package instructions or simply in a rice cooker. Shouldn't take longer than 20-30 minutes.

2. In the meantime, heat the rice vinegar in a small saucepan and stir with 1 tsp salt and 1 tsp sugar until the salt and sugar have dissolved. Place the finished sushi rice in a large bowl with the vinegar mixture and stir in well with a wooden spoon. Then set the sushi rice aside and let it cool.

3. Now the filling can be prepared: Peel the mango, cucumber and avocado and cut into strips.Cut the turkey breast into fine strips and fry in a pan with a little oil, salting and peppering.

4. Squeeze half a lemon for the cream. In a bowl, stir in the crème fraîche, cream cheese and 1 tablespoon of oil, add a little lemon juice, chili flakes, salt, pepper and sugar, depending on your taste, and mix. Chop peanuts and set aside in a bowl.

5. Provide all ingredients - sushi rice, cucumber, mango, avocado, peanuts, cream and arugula, as well as the bamboo mats with one nori sheet each.

6. Now it's time to fill and roll! To do this, dip your fingers in a bowl of water so that the rice does not stick to your fingers as much. Now distribute the sushi rice on the nori sheet. Cut out an inch. Spread a blob of the delicious cream in the middle of the seaweed sheet. Top with a few strips of turkey, cucumber, mango and avocado. Sprinkle with arugula and peanuts. Now drizzle the end of the algae leaf with water so that the nori leaf sticks to the end of the rolling when it is closed. Roll the sushi burrito from the bottom up. Press firmly on the roller. The finished sushi burrito can still be wrapped in baking paper or aluminum foil and cut in half diagonally. Place the soy sauce in a small bowl for dipping. Good Appetite!

SUSHI BALLS

INGREDIENTS FOR 1 PORTIONS

- 1 port of rice, sushi finished
- Wasabi paste
- 200 g of salmon, smoked, cut into pieces the size of postage stamps
- 1 point of shrimp
- 50 g of roe from the fly fish
- Pickled cucumber, thinly sliced
- 100 g of roast beef, cut into thin slices the size of postage stamps
- 100 g of tuna cut into pieces the size of postage stamps
- Radish, japanese, pickled, cut into postage-sized pieces

PREPARATION

Total time approx. 30 minutes

1. Halve the amount of rice. Spread a piece of cling film about 10x10 cm in size on the work surface and place a piece of smoked salmon in the middle. Spread a little wasabi on the salmon. Form 1 tablespoon sushi rice into a loose ball and place on top.

2. Lift and twist all 4 corners of the cling film to compress fish and rice into a tight ball. Do the same with the cucumber slices.

3. For the shrimp balls, place a shrimp in the middle of the cling film and put some fly fry in the bend. Form another tablespoon of rice into a loose ball, put on the shrimp and form a firm ball with the foil.

4. The finished balls can be kept in the cling film until shortly before serving.

5. Arrange on a plate and serve with soy sauce and pickled ginger.

CUCUMBER SUSHI

INGREDIENTS FOR 2 PORTIONS

- Cucumber (one as straight as possible)
- 75 g of rice (sushi or milk rice)
- 2 tbsp of vinegar (rice vinegar)
- ½ tsp of salt
- Wasabi paste or horseradish
- 100 g of smoked salmon
- 15 g of caviar
- Cress
- Sugar
- 200 ml of water, salted

PREPARATION

Total time approx. 30 minutes

1. Wash the rice cold repeatedly until the water remains as clear as possible. Then bring to the boil once in 150 ml - 200 ml of salt water, then cook in a low heat with the lid closed in about 10-15 minutes.

2. Season the warm rice with rice vinegar, salt and sugar and let it cool. For warm sushi, use the rice immediately without letting it cool down.

3. Wash and peel the cucumber. Halve lengthways and scrape out the core with a teaspoon. Brush the inside of the cucumber with wasabi paste or horseradish, then pour the rice into the cucumber halves. Cut everything into 2-3 cm diamonds. Put a little smoked salmon or a pinch of caviar on each piece and serve garnished with cress.

DITHMARSCHER SUSHI

INGREDIENTS FOR 6 PORTIONS

- Radish
- Kohlrabi
- Apple
- Pear
- ½ mackerel, smoked
- ¼ eel, (smoked eel)
- Matjes filet
- 12 shrimp, smoked

PREPARATION

Total time approx. 25 minutes

1. This recipe was quasi "obeying the need" in Dithmarschen and was extremely well received.

2. The ingredients are completely variable, you can use any solid smoked fish, but also smoked salmon or, for example, a mixture of crabs, mackerel whip and a dash of lemon. You can also vary vegetables or fruit, of course it must be a vegetable that can be eaten raw.

3. Preparation: Cut equal sized pieces of 2cm x 4cm from the fruit and / or vegetables.

4. Also cut different types of fish or seafood (by the way, the slightly salty matjes tastes great, for example, on canned pears!) Into pieces of the same size that fit on the vegetable pieces.

5. Now arrange the parts on a plate and use toothpicks instead of chopsticks for pricking.

OSHI SUSHI

INGREDIENTS FOR 8 PORTIONS

- 400 g of rice (sushi rice), ready prepared (see basic recipe)
- ¼ salad cucumber, cut lengthways
- 8 king prawns without head with shell
- 4 tbsp of sake
- 1 teaspoon of wasabi paste
- Salt

PREPARATION

Total time approx. 20 minutes

1. Line a baking tin with cling film.

2. Wash the shrimps, dry them, and fix them lengthways with a roulade needle. Bring some salted water to the boil with the sake in a saucepan. Switch off the hotplate and let the shrimp soak in the broth until they turn red. Peel and halve the shrimp and remove the intestine.

3. Wash the cucumber and halve lengthways. Remove the seeds and pat the cucumber halves dry. 5 Cut approximately 0.5 cm wide strips that are as long as the shape. Sprinkle the cucumber with a little sea salt, let it steep for approx. 30 min and pat dry again.

4. Brush the shrimp on the white inside with a little wasabi paste and place them side by side on the bottom of the mold so that the red outer skin comes to rest on the transparent film, cover with half of the sushi rice. Place the cucumber strips on the rice, press down lightly and cover with the rest of the rice. Fold the cling film over the rice so that everything is covered. With a second mold, a lid or the like. Cover, press gently and weigh down evenly with a weight so that the Oshi sushi is pressed evenly and firmly.

5. After 30-40 minutes, throw the Oshi Sushi out of the mold onto a board. Carefully remove the cling film and cut the Oshi Sushi into 8 parts with a sharp knife.

SUSHI SANDWICH

INGREDIENTS FOR 1 PORTIONS

- 100 g of tofu
- Soy sauce
- 1 teaspoon of chili flakes
- Ginger
- Garlic cloves
- 2 nori sheets
- 70 g of sushi rice
- 30 g of avocado
- 6 g of baby spinach
- 50 g of red cabbage
- 30 ml of rice vinegar
- 5 ml of maple syrup
- Sea-salt
- ½ garlic cloves

PREPARATION

Total time approx. 1 hour 25 minutes

1. Marinate the tofu with the soy sauce, the clove of garlic, 1 teaspoon chili flakes and a little chopped ginger. Meanwhile cook the sushi rice according to the package instructions. Fry the marinated tofu in a non-stick pan for about 3 minutes on all sides.

2. Peel the avocado, remove the core and cut into slices. Wash the baby spinach and pat dry with kitchen paper.

3. For the red cabbage salad, wash 30 g of red cabbage and cut into narrow strips. Put the rice vinegar, maple syrup, a little sea salt and ½ clove of garlic with a little water in a saucepan and bring to a boil over medium heat. Pour the warm dressing over the red cabbage, mix well, cool and let it soak.

4. Use a small bowl to bring the sushi rice into a square shape, place it in the middle of the nori sheet and place the baby spinach leaves on it. Now press a little red cabbage salad onto the spinach with a fork and spread a few slices of the avocado on top. Finally cut the marinated tofu in half lengthways, cut smaller if necessary and place on the avocado slices. When arranging all ingredients, make sure that they are placed as close together as possible and layered in the shape of a square. Now moisten the fingertips with a little water and glue the corners of the sheet together in the middle of the sandwich so that the ingredients are well wrapped in the nori sheet. Moisten again with water if a corner of the sheet should not stick immediately.

5. Halve the sandwich and serve with soy sauce.

VEGGIE ONIGIRI

INGREDIENTS FOR 12 PORTIONS

- 250 g of sushi rice
- ½ tsp of salt
- 1 teaspoon of sugar
- 1 shot of sake
- 1 smaller broccoli
- 1 handful corn
- 1 handful gouda, grated
- 1 cup of cream cheese
- Cucumber
- Avocado
- 1 nori sheet

PREPARATION

Total time approx. 1 hour 40 minutes

1. Cook the sushi rice according to the instructions, e.g. Bring to the boil, cook for 10 minutes on a low flame, remove from the stove for 10 minutes and let cook.

2. While the sushi is cooking rice, prepare the broccoli so that it has time to cool down. Peel the avocado and cut it into small pieces. Peel the cucumber and cut it into small cubes.

3. Place the salt, sugar and sake in a cold bowl (metal, unpainted wood or stone) and mix, then add the sushi rice.

4. Let the sushi rice cool, e.g. Put the rice in a bowl in cold water or in the refrigerator and best stir again and again, then it cools down faster.

5. Press a teaspoon-sized mass of the cooled sushi rice flat in your hand, then add any cold ingredients: - a level teaspoon of cream cheese and three small pieces of avocado

6. Some cream cheese with a few cubes of cucumber. Some corn with Gouda, a few florets with broccoli and some cream cheese.

7. Then flatten a small amount of rice in the other hand and place it on top to seal the onigiri.

8. Both the corn and the broccoli filling are a bit of a mess, so it's best not to seal the onigiri but to mix the sushi rice with the filling in hand.

9. The cucumber and the Philadelphia should also be mixed in a bowl, this makes preparation easier.

10. Press the onigiri into small shapes (traditionally triangular) and press an approximately thumb-sized piece of nori sheet to one side. This is mainly intended not to get your fingers dirty when consumed.

ONIGIRI WITH SALMON AND CHICKEN

INGREDIENTS FOR 2 PORTIONS

- 2 cups of rice (short grain rice)
- 100 g of salmon, smoked, or very fresh
- 100 g of chicken breast fillet
- 4 nori sheets
- 3 tbsp of vinegar (sushi-zu), ready-made sushi vinegar for seasoning the rice
- Wasabi paste
- Soy sauce, for dipping
- Mayonnaise
- Spice mix (furikake)

PREPARATION

Total time approx. 30 minutes

1. Rinse the short grain rice in a sieve until the water remains clear. Place in a saucepan with 4 cups of water. Bring rice to a boil over high heat. As soon as foam in the pot threatens to rise, turn off the stove and let the rice rest on the warm stove for 15 minutes. Very important: While the rice is boiling and then resting, never remove the lid. Determining when the rice is cooking is best done with a glass-lid pot.

2. Season the still hot rice with the sushi and let it cool.

3. In the meantime, dice the chicken breast fillet, season and fry. Dice the salmon. Cut each nori sheet into 5 strips of equal size.

4. Now form balls out of the rice. The easiest way is with an onigiri shape, which comes in different shapes and sizes. Fill rice balls in the middle with salmon or chicken. Add a swab of mayonnaise to fill as you like.

5. Brush the finished onigiri with a little wasabi paste and wrap each with a strip of nori.

TOAST SUSHI ROLLS

INGREDIENTS FOR 1 PORTIONS

- 500 g of toasted bread (whole grain)
- 200 g of cream cheese
- Milk
- Salt
- Pepper
- 1 cucumber
- 1 carrot
- 1 salami

PREPARATION

Total time approx. 20 minutes

1. Debark the toasted bread, then roll it out very flat with the rolling pin. Whip cream cheese with 1-2 tablespoons of milk and season with salt and pepper.

2. Cut the other ingredients into pens about 1-2 cm thick. The length of the pens depends on the toasted bread - they should be a little longer than this is wide. Spread the cream cheese thinly on the toast slices and top with a cucumber, carrot and salami stick. Then roll up as tight as possible - the best way to do this is with a sushi mat. Cut sushi of approx. 4 cm each with a very sharp knife with a smooth cutting edge.

3. Filling variations:
    - Only cucumber, only carrot or only avocado
    - smoked salmon
    - Egg and herb spread (instead of cream cheese) and cooked ham
    - Bell pepper - Cream cheese without salt and pepper and jam, such as strawberry, raspberry etc.

TOAST ROLLS WITH SALMON CREAM CHEESE FILLING

INGREDIENTS FOR 1 PORTIONS

- 6 discs of toasted bread, whole grain
- 150 g of cream cheese
- 200 g of smoked salmon
- Pepper
- Dill
- Horseradish, optional

PREPARATION

Total time approx. 1 hour 20 minutes

1. First cut the rind off the toast slices, then roll the toast slices flat with a pasta roll (alternatively glass bottle). Spread the cream cheese thinly on the toast slices and top them with smoked salmon. Season to taste and add horseradish if necessary.
2. Roll up the toast slices, then wrap in aluminum or plastic wrap. Then place the rolls in the refrigerator for at least 1 hour so that the toast becomes softer and easier to cut. For serving, they are cut into 6 to 8 pieces (just like sushi).

DISHES

TUNA TARTARE ON AVOCADO CREAM

INGREDIENTS FOR 2 PORTIONS

For the fish:

- 250 g of tuna, frozen or sushi quality
- Shallot
- ¼ cucumber
- Oil
- Salt and pepper

For the salad:

- 50 g of lamb's lettuce
- Pomegranate

For the dip:

- Avocado, ripe
- Lemon juice

- Salt

Also: (for the parmesan crackers)

- 50 g of parmesan
- Salt and pepper

Furthermore:

- Horseradish
- Wasabi paste
- Some stems of cress

PREPARATION

Total time approx. 1 hour 3 minutes

1. Cut the tuna very small, as well as the shallots and the cucumber. Mix the three ingredients together, season with salt, pepper and a little neutral oil and stir well.

2. Chop the parmesan finely, add a little salt and pepper and spread it on a baking sheet lined with baking paper. Bake in the oven at 200 ° C for approx. 8 minutes until the cheese has combined and is golden yellow. Let the cheese cool and set aside. This can also be prepared very well hours in advance.

3. Wash the lamb's lettuce well and "pulp" the seeds from the pomegranate.

4. Puree the avocado with a blender and add a little lemon juice and salt.

5. Now arrange the avocado cream on the plate and the tuna mixture using a serving ring, fill up the cream. Arrange the lamb's lettuce with the pomegranate seeds, decorate a dollop of horseradish and wasabi, garnish the whole thing with cress and add a little of the Parmesan pieces.

6. It goes with fresh baguette.

SPICY TUNA TARTARE

INGREDIENTS FOR 4 PORTIONS

- 2 tsp of heaped ginger, fresh, finely chopped or grated
- 100 ml of vegetable oil
- 400 g of tuna, sushi quality
- 2 tbsp of coriander green, finely chopped
- Chili pepper, seeded and finely chopped
- 1 tbsp of spring onion, finely chopped
- 3 tsp of lime juice
- Sea-salt
- Pepper
- 1 tomato, peeled and seeded

PREPARATION

Total time approx. 1 day 20 minutes

1. Soak the ginger in oil the day before and leave in the fridge. Cut the tuna into small cubes and place in a cold bowl.

2. Mix the chopped chili pepper, the spring onion, 3 teaspoons of lime juice and 4 teaspoons of the ginger oil with the pieces of ginger with a tablespoon of coriander. Salt and pepper.

3. Place in the middle of the plates using serving rings. Drizzle the remaining ginger oil around the tartare, put the finely chopped tomato pieces on top, then the rest of the coriander. Drizzle with lime juice.

TUNA TARTARE WITH CORIANDER PESTO

INGREDIENTS FOR 4 PORTIONS

- 1 bunch coriander
- 50 g of parmesan
- Olive oil
- 2 toes of garlic
- ½ tsp of salt
- 1 shot of gin, dry or wormwood
- 1 tbsp of lemon juice or lime juice
- Soy sauce
- 150 g of tuna, fresher

PREPARATION

Total time approx. 20 minutes

1. Scrape the fresh tuna off the whole piece with a normal tablespoon so that you get a coarse tartare. Mix this well with lemon juice, a little olive oil, gin and 1 - 1.5 tablespoons of soy sauce and, ideally, keep cool and covered.

2. Roughly chop the coriander and garlic for the pesto. If the parmesan is not grated, grate it. Fill with the pine nuts and salt in a tall container and chop with a hand blender. Fill up with olive oil until a mass with the consistency of toothpaste is created. Mix these in a ratio of 1: 3 from pesto to tartare with the tuna tartare and season with soy sauce.

3. As a variation, you can also replace about a quarter of the coriander with Thai basil or refine the tartare with some finely chopped ginger.

4. The rest of the pesto is kept in a closed container in the refrigerator for at least a week and goes well with pasta or starters.

REFINED TUNA TARTARE

INGREDIENTS FOR 6 PORTIONS

- 500 g of tuna, sushi-quality fillets
- 3 m of tomatoes
- Snake cucumber
- 3 tbsp of soy sauce
- 1 tsp of chili powder, red
- 1 bunch of coriander
- 1 splash of lemon juice
- 3 tbsp of olive oil, virgin
- 6 discs of pumpernickel
- 100 g of cream cheese e.g. Philadelphia

PREPARATION

Total time approx. 4 hours

1. Wash the tuna fillet, pat dry and place in the freezer for 5 hours. Cut this fillet, which is not completely frozen, with a very sharp knife into very thin slices (2 - 3 mm) and then process these slices into very small cubes using longitudinal and cross-sections. Due to the frozen condition, the fish can be worked very well with a knife.

2. Slice the tomatoes in a cross shape and place in boiling water for 1 - 2 minutes, then skin and quarter. Lift out the core casing with a large tablespoon and cut the tomato meat into small cubes (similar size to the tuna fillet).

3. Process the cucumber with a peeler and cut into two lengthways. Here too, scrape out the core casing with a large tablespoon and then cut the cucumber meat into small cubes similar to the tomatoes and fillet.

4. Clean the bunch of coriander under running water, shake off the water and shred with a 4 or 5-blade herb scissors. Put everything that has been chopped up so far with the remaining ingredients in a large mixing bowl and mix at low speed with a hand mixer with a dough hook.

5. Put the tartare in a container and let it steep in the refrigerator for 2-3 hours.

6. Just take it out of the fridge just before serving, put everything in a large sieve, press something from the top with a cellar or similar so that the resulting free liquid can drain off. On large flat plates with serving rings, cut round slices out of the pumpernickel slices and fill the tartare in portions in the rings, press on a little with a very thin layer of cream cheese and decorate with a sheet of coriander. Lift off the serving rings and decorate the plate with a few drops of soy sauce.

SALMON TARTARE WITH LEMON CREAM

INGREDIENTS FOR 4 PORTIONS

- 400 g of salmon fillet, sushi quality
- 200 g of smoked salmon
- 1 bar of leek
- Garlic
- 1½ tsp of honey
- 2 tbsp of olive oil
- 150 g of crème fraiche cheese
- 4 tsp of caviar (salmon)
- Cress
- Lemon, organic
- Salt and pepper

PREPARATION

Total time approx. 20 minutes

1. Finely dice the two types of salmon and finely dice the garlic.

2. Cut the leek in half into very thin half rings.

3. Mix everything with a marinade made from honey, olive oil and half the juice of the lemon and the grated lemon peel. Season with salt and pepper if desired. Season the crème fraiche with the remaining lemon juice and salt and pepper.

4. Arrange the tartare in metal rings or large biscuit cutters, spread the lemon cream on top. Garnish with cress. A little fresh baguette may also be enough.

TUNA CARPACCIO

INGREDIENTS FOR 4 PORTIONS

- 125 ml of oil
- 60 ml of lime juice
- 2 tbsp of fish sauce
- ¼ tsp of pepper, black, freshly ground
- Sugar
- 400 g of tuna, sushi - quality
- 3 tbsp of coriander green, roughly chopped

PREPARATION

Total time approx. 15 minutes

1. Cut the tuna into very fine slices, freeze if necessary beforehand. Prepare the dressing, pour half on a plate. Place the tuna slices on top of each other and cover with the rest of the dressing.
2. Marinate in the refrigerator for at least 30 minutes.
3. Sprinkle with coriander before serving.

HAND CHEESE

INGREDIENTS FOR 4 PORTIONS

- 200 g of cheese (hand cheese) without caraway
- Shallot, chopped
- 2 tbsp of vinegar (sushi vinegar)
- 2 tbsp of cider
- 1 tbsp of peanut oil
- 1 teaspoon of peppercorns (cubeb pepper)
- ¼ tsp of cayenne pepper
- 1 pinch of salt and pepper, black from the mill

PREPARATION

Total time approx. 30 minutes

1. Cut the hand cheese into slices and place in a bowl. Sprinkle the chopped shallots over it.
2. Mix the remaining ingredients into a marinade and bring to the boil briefly. Pour hot over the hand cheese. Let cool for 20 minutes.
3. Spread on plates and serve sprinkled with black pepper.

PANGASIUS ON FENNEL SALAD IN ORANGE VINAIGRETTE

INGREDIENTS FOR 4 PORTIONS

- 500 g of fish fillet (pangasius fillet), ready to cook
- 1 toe of garlic
- 1 branch of thyme
- Oil, for frying
- 2 tuber fennels
- Orange, organic
- 3 tbsp of vinegar, (sushi vinegar)
- 1 tbsp of oil, (orange oil)
- 5 tbsp of olive oil
- Salt
- Pepper

PREPARATION

Total time approx. 30 minutes

1. If necessary, finely grate the orange peel or tear the zests and mix with the olive oil to produce an "orange oil".

2. Peel the oranges, remove the fillets with a small knife and set aside. Squeeze the juice of the remaining orange and collect in a bowl. First add vinegar, salt, sugar and pepper while stirring until the spices have dissolved. Now slowly add the oils (orange oil and olive oil) and stir into a dressing.

3. Set fennel green aside for decoration. Clean fennel and cut into thin slices, better plan. Put in the bowl and marinate with the dressing. Add the orange fillets.

4. If necessary, portion the fish. Fry and cook briefly on both sides in a pan with the oil, the pressed garlic and the thyme. Season with salt and pepper.

5. Serving: First arrange the fennel salad with the orange fillets on a plate. Place the fish on top and decorate with fennel green. Good Appetite!

MARINATED TUNA ON A NORI AND RICE BED

INGREDIENTS FOR 2 PORTIONS

- Tuna fillet
- 4 nori sheets
- 2 bars of leek
- 3 bars of spring onions
- Carrot
- 4 tbsp of sesame
- 3 toes of garlic
- 10 tbsp of soy sauce
- 6 tbsp of sake
- ½ tsp of sambal oelek
- 2 teaspoons of wasabi paste
- 1 tbsp of sugar
- 125 g of rice, sushi
- 2 tbsp of rice vinegar
- Oil, (peanut oil)

PREPARATION

Total time approx. 1 hour 20 minutes

1. Mix the soy sauce, sake and sugar in a bowl until the sugar has completely dissolved. Then marinate the tuna fillets (preferably sushi quality) in a closed bowl for at least 30 minutes. In the meantime, clean the vegetables and cut them into small slices.

2. Roast sesame seeds in a pan (without adding fat) while stirring constantly until they turn brown. Then take out and set aside.

3. Remove the tuna fillets from the marinade and set aside. Place the marinade in a wok (or a suitable pan) and add the wasabi paste and sambal oelek. Heat the liquid on a low setting and add the vegetables (except the garlic). Let it simmer for about 20 minutes.

4. Cook the sushi rice for 15 minutes according to the instructions, drain, add rice vinegar and leave covered for another 15 minutes.

5. Fry the tuna fillets in peanut oil on both sides for about 90 seconds and then turn both sides in the sesame seeds. Then add the garlic to the oil and roast while stirring. Do not let it burn!

6. Divide the nori sheet and place one half on each plate. Then moisten slightly. Place the rice in the middle of the nori sheet and distribute it about the size of the tuna fillet.

7. Place the tuna on the rice bed, put the garlic on the tuna and spread vegetables with liquid around the rice bed.

ASIAN COLESLAW WITH GLAZED SALMON FILLET

INGREDIENTS FOR 4 PORTIONS

- 800 g of white cabbage
- 1 tbsp of salt
- 2 tbsp of sugar
- Lemon, the juice of it
- 200 g of carrot
- 6 stems mint
- Sesame oil, toasted
- 25 g of ginger, (sushi ginger) pickled
- 2 teaspoons of soy sauce
- 3 tbsp of honey
- Chili sauce, (thai sweet chili sauce)
- Salmon fillet
- Oil, for frying

PREPARATION

Total time approx. 30 minutes

1. Roughly grate the white cabbage. Mix with salt and sugar and knead vigorously with your hands. Squeeze out the lemon juice and add it. Peel the carrots and grate them roughly. Wash the mint, dry it, pluck the leaves and cut them finely. Mix everything with the herb and season with the sesame oil.

2. Finely chop the ginger and mix with soy sauce, honey and the chilli sauce. Heat the oil in a pan and fry the salmon until crispy on both sides. Turn off the stove and spread the sauce over the salmon. Turn several times and let glaze briefly.

3. Arrange salmon with the coleslaw.

SIMPLE POKE BOWL

INGREDIENTS FOR 2 PORTIONS

- 1 cup of jasmine rice
- 300 g of salmon (sushi salmon) or smoked salmon
- 1 small can of pineapple
- 50 g of algae, steamed
- 1 small cucumber
- Bell pepper, red
- Tomatoes
- Avocado
- 1 tbsp of sesame
- 2 tbsp of soy sauce
- 4 tbsp of sesame oil
- 1 small piece of ginger

PREPARATION

Total time approx. 20 minutes

1. The Poke bowl is a mixture of sushi and Buddha bowl, can be varied to your heart's content and refrigerator contents and is super healthy!

2. Simply cook the rice according to the package instructions, let it cool a little and spread it over 2 bowls. Then arrange the finely chopped vegetables on top. Prepare a dressing from sesame oil, soy sauce and grated ginger and pour over it. Sprinkle with sesame seeds and serve.

TAMAGOYAKI SUSHI OMELETTE

INGREDIENTS FOR 2 PORTIONS

- 6 eggs
- 50 ml of dashi
- Water
- 1 tbsp of sake
- 1 teaspoon of mirin
- 1 tbsp of soy sauce, good quality
- 20 g of sugar
- 1 pinch of salt
- 2 tbsp of oil

PREPARATION

Total time approx. 30 minutes

1. Bring the dashi, sake, mirin and sugar to the boil for 1 minute so that everything mixes better and the alcohol evaporates, then let it cool. Beat the eggs with a little salt and the soy sauce until they are foamy, then mix the dashi mass, which has cooled down, with it.

2. Now you need a rectangular, Japanese pan, but you can also try to prepare a Japanese omelet in round pans. You could later cut everything into a large rectangle and use the trimmed edges for something else.

3. Spread a little oil in the pan and add about 1/4 of the egg mass. If it sticks to the floor, beat a quarter of the area from the outside in, folding it like a piece of paper for a letter. Then fold the 2nd and 3rd quarters over the next one. Now spread some oil on the free bottom of the pan again and fill thinly with egg mass. Fold them, starting with the egg mass already folded, in the same way as before. Repeat these two steps two more times until the egg mass is used up. This creates a relatively increased role. Let the roll slide on a board, degrease with kitchen paper on the outside and cut into even slices of approx. 1-2 cm.

4. Either eat immediately or use at room temperature for nigiri sushi. The omelet tastes pure when cooled.

INARI SUSHI

INGREDIENTS FOR 4 PORTIONS

- 220 g of rice, sushi
- 500 ml of water
- 2 tbsp of sesame, japanese, white
- 2 tbsp of rice vinegar
- 1 tbsp of sugar
- 1 tbsp of mirin
- 1 teaspoon of salt
- 12 tofu bags (inari bags)

PREPARATION

Total time approx. 1 hour 40 minutes

1. Wash rice in a colander under running water, drain well. Bring water and rice to a boil. Reduce the heat and simmer for 4-5 minutes without the lid until the water is absorbed. Put the lid on and let stand for a further 4-5 minutes on low heat, then remove from the heat and let it swell in the closed pot for 10 minutes.

2. Roast the sesame seeds in a dry pan until golden brown for 3-4 minutes and gently swirl them in between; then take it out immediately.

3. Mix the vinegar, sugar, mirin and salt and add to the rice. Stir with a wooden spoon until the rice has cooled.

4. Carefully detach and open the Inari bags. Fill each with 1 tablespoon of rice. Sprinkle the rice with toasted sesame seeds, then squeeze the bag closed. Arrange on a platter and serve.

NOTE:
- Inari bags are stuffed bags made from deep fried tofu. You can buy them in Asian grocery stores.

SUSHI PATTIES

INGREDIENTS FOR 2 PORTIONS

- 2 cups of rice, (normal long grain rice) or at will
- 2 cups of millet, (golden millet)
- 4 nori sheets
- 1 teaspoon of broth, instant (without yeast)
- Egg
- 1 teaspoon of flour
- Soy sauce
- Olive oil, or sesame oil
- Water
- Breadcrumbs

PREPARATION

Total time approx. 1 hour

1. Place 2 espresso cups full of rice and millet in a saucepan, fill with 3 espresso cups of water and add a teaspoon of broth powder, let simmer for 10 minutes (with the lid on), then set the hob down and let it swell again on the hob for 15 minutes.

2. Cut the nori sheet into fine strips (best with scissors) and add to the rice and millet mixture with the egg and a teaspoon of flour (to bind), mix well. If the mass is too liquid (it should be a firm paste), you can add some breadcrumbs. Those who do not suffer from HI can still season with a little soy sauce, otherwise add a little salt (try the mass beforehand).

3. Heat some sesame oil in a pan (please use olive oil for HI) (medium heat) and add 4-5 piles into the pan with the help of 2 tablespoons, press a little flat, fry on both sides until golden brown.

4. It goes very well with (very un-Asian) cucumber salad.

5. If you like, you can of course play with other spices, but the nori leaves have their own taste that you shouldn't "kill" with spices that are too strong.

VEGAN GOLUBTSI ON BRAISED VEGETABLES

INGREDIENTS FOR 1 PORTIONS

For the parcels:

- 8 sheets of white cabbage
- 70 g of sushi rice
- 40 g of sliced (pea cutlet), alternatively soybean cutlet, fine
- 1 teaspoon of vegetable broth powder
- ½ tsp of smoked salt
- ½ tsp of pepper
- Bay leaf
- 1 small pickles

For the vegetables:

- ½ onion
- Leek stick
- 1 small carrot
- ½ smaller celery

- ½ pepper
- 2 m in size tomatoes
- 1 teaspoon of vegetable broth powder
- ½ tsp of salt
- ½ tsp of pepper
- 1 teaspoon of paprika powder
- Cornstarch
- 1 tbsp of oil for frying

PREPARATION

Total time approx. 2 hours

1. Blanch the white cabbage leaves in salted water until the leaves are soft and slightly transparent. Drain the white cabbage leaves and let them cool.

2. Simmer the sushi rice with the vegetable stock powder, salt, pepper and the bay leaf in sufficient water according to the package for approx. 10 minutes. Stir occasionally and add the pea cutlet. Dice the pickled cucumber and add to the rice mince mixture. Let the pea cutlet go with the rice for a few minutes. The liquid should be completely absorbed. Now let the mixture cool and remove the bay leaf.

3. While the mass cools, wash, clean and cut the vegetables into small cubes. Put the oil in a saucepan or roaster, fry the vegetables in it until it has some color and season with the specified spices. Then add water to the vegetables until almost covered and simmer.

4. In the meantime, put the rice-chop mixture on the cabbage leaves, roll once, fold in the sides and continue rolling up. Place the golubtsi on the vegetables with the open side down. Let the cabbage rolls simmer on a low setting for about 45 minutes with the lid closed. At the end of the cooking time, tie the vegetables with a little cornstarch.

SUSHI BOWL

INGREDIENTS FOR 4 PORTIONS

- 500 g of sushi rice
- 50 ml of rice wine
- 4 avocados
- Cucumber
- 1 can of ginger, pickled, approx.100g
- 250 g of salmon, smoked or cooked
- 150 g of shrimp, cooked
- 4 nori sheets
- Handful sesame
- Soy sauce
- Mayonnaise
- Sriracha sauce

PREPARATION

Total time approx. 2 hours 40 minutes

1. Cook the sushi rice with rice wine according to the package instructions, then let it cool and chill.

2. Cut avocados, cucumber, salmon, shrimp and nori leaves into small pieces.

3. Drizzle the rice with soy sauce and garnish with all the ingredients.

4. Mix a new sauce from mayonnaise and sriracha sauce and stain all ingredients with it.

JAPANESE SEAWEED SALAD

INGREDIENTS FOR 4 PORTIONS

- 1 bag of wakame, dried seaweed (in a bag are 56 grams)
- 3 tbsp of vinegar, (sushi, rice)
- 3 tbsp of sesame oil
- 1 tbsp of lime juice
- 1 tbsp of ginger, freshly grated
- 1 tbsp of sugar
- 1 toe of garlic, pressed
- 2 tbsp of coriander green, finely chopped
- ½ tbsp of chili powder
- 1 tbsp of sesame

PREPARATION

Total time approx. 1 hour 20 minutes

1. Pour seaweed on with hot water and leave for 10 min. to let go.

2. Prepare the sauce:

3. Mix all of the above ingredients (except the seaweed and sesame seeds) in a small bowl until smooth. Season with the chili powder depending on the hotness.

4. Drain the seaweed and wring it out a little. Now simply fold the drained kelp under the sauce and sprinkle sesame seeds over it as you like. Let it brew for approx. 1 hour, preferably in the refrigerator.

SUSHI SALAD

INGREDIENTS FOR 2 PORTIONS

- 100 g of sushi rice, drier
- 150 ml of water
- 25 ml of rice vinegar
- 1 tbsp of sugar
- Salt
- 120 g of shrimp, pre-cooked
- 100 g of salmon, raw, fresh or frozen
- Cucumber
- 4 nori leaves (roasted seaweed)
- 1 tbsp of ginger, pickled, drained
- Lime
- ½ tsp of wasabi paste
- 1 tbsp of soy sauce
- 1 tbsp of sweet chili sauce

PREPARATION

Total time approx. 1 hour 15 minutes

1. Wash the rice and gently simmer in a saucepan covered with water for 15 minutes (if necessary, add water), remove from the heat and let it swell again for 30 minutes.

2. Mix rice vinegar, 1 teaspoon sugar and 1/4 teaspoon salt and mix into the rice.

3. Peel, core and cut the cucumber into small cubes. Cut the nori sheets into small pieces (it works best with kitchen scissors). Also cut the salmon into small pieces. Then carefully mix everything - including the shrimp and ginger - with the cooled rice.

4. Squeeze the limes. Mix the wasabi, lime juice, soy sauce and sweet chili sauce and the remaining sugar and mix this dressing with the salad. Chill again and let it go through.

5. Do not store the salad for long as there is raw salmon in it.

JAPANESE ONION SAUCE WITH CABBAGE AND SHRIMP

INGREDIENTS FOR 2 PORTIONS

For the sauce:

- 1 m of onion
- 2 garlic cloves
- 2 tbsp of honey
- 4 tbsp of soy sauce, light
- 4 tbsp of sherry, dry
- 1 tbsp of tabasco or red pepper sauce
- 6 tbsp of sesame oil
- 2 tbsp of oyster sauce

For the salad:

- 1 smaller chinese cabbage
- Carrot
- ¼ cucumber
- 100 g of shrimp, cooked
- Sesame

PREPARATION

Total time approx. 15 minutes

1. For the sauce, roughly chop the onion, peel and quarter the garlic. Put in a blender with all ingredients and puree to a smooth sauce.

2. Cut the Chinese cabbage into small pieces, remove the hard pieces and the stalk, blanch in salted water for 5 minutes, drain, quench with ice-cold water and let cool. Peel and cut the carrot so that you can cut 3 - 4 cm long thin sticks. Halve the cucumber, remove the seeds and also cut into 3 - 4 cm long thin sticks. Mix the cooled Chinese cabbage with about ¾ of the sauce and fill in small bowls. Decorate with carrot, cucumber sticks and shrimp, pour the remaining sauce over it and sprinkle with sesame seeds.

3. Anyone who likes to eat sushi should have stumbled across a salad made with such a sauce. What exactly you take for a salad is of course a matter of taste, alternatives to Chinese cabbage would be iceberg or romaine lettuce, carrots and cucumber always look good in it and sesame is actually a must.

PASTA SALAD WITH ROASTED BROCCOLI AND PEANUT-SILK TOFU SAUCE

INGREDIENTS FOR 6 PORTIONS

- 80 ml of soy sauce, sweet (kikkoman sushi & sashimi)
- 150 ml of vegetable broth
- 100 g of tofu (silk tofu)
- 1 teaspoon of tabasco
- Garlic cloves
- 100 g of peanuts, roasted, salted
- 250 g of broccoli
- 4 tbsp of sesame oil
- 150 g of salad (lettuce hearts)
- 200 g of pasta (spaghetti), vegan
- Salt water
- 1 teaspoon of sesame oil
- 3 tbsp of roasted onions
- Salt
- Coriander green (4 - 6 stems)

PREPARATION

Total time approx. 30 minutes

1. For the peanut sauce, puree the broth, the silk tofu, the chili sauce, the peeled garlic and 50 g peanuts (no more!) With a blender or a blender and add a little salt if necessary. The flavor of the broth and soy sauce is enough for my taste.

2. Cut the broccoli into thin slices, salt and fry in a wok or large pan in hot oil over medium heat for about 5 minutes. Meanwhile, cut the lettuce hearts into fine strips.

3. Cook the pasta in salted water according to the package instructions, cool under cold water and mix in a sieve with the sesame oil. If you want to eat it warm, leave out the step with the cold water!

4. Roughly chop the remaining 50 g of peanuts, then mix all the ingredients with the peanut sauce. Finally sprinkle the whole thing with the fried onions and serve (if you like) with plucked coriander leaves.

SUSHI BOWL WITH TAMAGOYAKI

INGREDIENTS FOR 2 PORTIONS

- 150 g of round grain rice
- ½ cucumber
- Bell pepper, red
- Carrot
- Avocado
- 2 tbsp of sesame
- 5 tbsp of rice vinegar
- 2 tbsp of sesame oil
- 2 tbsp of soy sauce
- Ginger powder
- Egg
- 3 tbsp of sake
- 1 teaspoon of soy sauce
- 2 teaspoons of sugar
- Salt

PREPARATION

Total time approx. 45 minutes

1. Prepare the rice according to the package instructions. Meanwhile wash the vegetables. Cut the peppers and the cucumber into thin strips and the avocado into slices. Peel the carrot and cut into thin strips with the peeler.

2. Heat some sesame oil in a pan. Beat the eggs in a bowl and whisk. Add 3 tablespoons of sake, 1 teaspoon of soy sauce, 2 teaspoons of sugar and a little salt and stir well.

3. Put 1/3 of the egg mixture into the hot pan. As soon as the egg freezes, roll it up to the middle. Put the egg mass on the vacated area again and make sure that it runs under the rolled egg.

4. Wait for the egg to freeze and roll in again - this time in the other direction. Place the rest of the egg mass on the vacated area, wait until it stops and roll up completely.

5. Take the rolled omelet out of the pan and cut into slices. Set everything aside.

6. Mix 5 tablespoons of rice vinegar, 2 tablespoons of sesame oil and 2 tablespoons of soy sauce and season with the ginger powder. Toast the sesame seeds in a pan without oil.

7. Spread the rice on bowls (e.g. cereal bowls) and garnish with the vegetables and omelet. Spread the vinegar-oil-sauce mixture over it. Finally sprinkle the roasted sesame over it and serve.

BEEF WITH ONIONS AND SUGAR SNAP PEAS FROM THE WOK

INGREDIENTS FOR 6 PORTIONS

- 1.4 kg of beef fillet
- 3 tbsp of vinegar (japanese sushi vinegar)
- 4 tsp of heaped food starch
- 8 tsp of soy sauce
- 2 tbsp of honey
- 1 bottle peanut oil
- 6 large carrots
- 4 large vegetable onions
- 6 fret spring onions
- 200 g of sugar snap
- 1 large chinese bulb of garlic
- 1 glass of bamboo shoot
- 2 pinches of chili flakes
- 2 teaspoons of pepper, freshly ground black
- 1 bunch leaf parsley, fresh
- ¼ liter of broth
- ¼ liter of cream
- 350 g of basmati rice, approx. 2 large cups

PREPARATION

Total time approx. 1 hour 20 minutes

1. Remove tendons and fat from the fillet of beef, cut the meat into thin 3 cm strips and place in a container. Mix the sushi vinegar, 4 tablespoons of peanut oil, the soy sauce and honey, and the cornstarch in a bowl with a hand whisk. Then mix well with the strips of meat in the container and put the meat in the fridge for 1.5 hours to marinate.

2. Cook the rice as usual.

3. In the meantime, cut the carrots into 5 cm strips, peel, cut in half and quarter the butcher onions and remove the individual onion skins. Wash the sugar snap peas, cut off the ends of the stems and cut the pods in half. Peel and chop the bulb of garlic. Wash the parsley and chop it with a sharp knife. Cut the spring onions into 0.5 cm rings.

4. Heat a shot of peanut oil in the wok (the oil is hot enough if bubbles form on a wooden spoon). Sear the meat in several stages for two minutes, remove from the wok and let it rest.

5. Fry the carrots in a wok with a little peanut oil and remove them, then add the sugar pods, onion skin and spring onions and fry. Add half of the garlic and fry. Add the chili flakes and the bamboo shoots.

6. Now the meat can be mixed with the resulting juice and all ingredients in the wok, only add the black ground pepper with the remaining garlic at the end. Simmer briefly on a low heat, pour in the broth, a little soy sauce and a little dash of cream, then combine with a little brown cornstarch as you like.

7. Serve with parsley sprinkled with the rice.

SASHIMI BOWL

INGREDIENTS FOR 4 PORTIONS

- 500 g of sushi rice
- 80 ml of rice vinegar
- Avocado
- 4 spring onions
- Cucumber
- 4 tbsp of sesame seeds, toasted
- 250 g of salmon, raw, in sushi quality
- 250 g of tuna, raw, in sushi quality
- 100 ml of soy sauce, mild
- 4 tsp of wasabi paste

PREPARATION

Total time approx. 1 hour 35 minutes

1. Cook the sushi rice according to the package instructions. Then pour the rice vinegar over it. Refrigerate.

2. Cut all other ingredients into small pieces and prepare them.

3. Fill four bowls with the rice to serve. Spread the remaining ingredients on the rice and sprinkle with toasted sesame.

4. Serve with soy sauce and wasabi paste.

5. Pickled ginger and freshly chopped coriander go well with it. If you like, you can also add fresh cubed mango to the bowl and add a dash of lime to the avocado.

POKÉ BOWL

INGREDIENTS FOR 3 PORTIONS

- 2 discs of tuna
- 1 cup of sushi rice (approx. 200 - 250 ml)
- 1 cup of soybeans, fresh (approx. 200 - 250 ml), frozen
- 1 tbsp of sesame, black, toasted
- 150 g of wakame (algae salad goma wakame), frozen, seasoned
- ½ chili pepper, fresh, red, medium hot
- Ginger, not too fresh
- 15 tbsp of teriyaki sauce
- Spring onions

PREPARATION

Total time approx. 2 hours 50 minutes

1. Cook the sushi rice according to the package instructions, then let it cool in a flat bowl.

2. Thaw and fry the tuna, then salt and pepper and let cool. Then tear into bite-size pieces. Drizzle with half of the teriyaki sauce, place in a Tupper jar and chill for at least 2 hours.

3. Cook frozen soybeans until they are bite-proof in salted water for about 5 - 10 minutes, then drain and let cool.

4. Cut the chili and spring onion into the finest rings and the ginger into fine cubes. Simply thaw the seaweed salad.

5. Then e.g. Use mason jars for portioning. First pour rice into a glass, then pour in the seaweed salad and the other ingredients, the tuna last. Sprinkle with the sesame seeds and drizzle with 2 - 3 tablespoons of teriyaki sauce.

JAPANESE STYLE BOWL

INGREDIENTS FOR 2 PORTIONS

- Cod fillet with skin
- 300 g of sushi rice
- 2 small spring onions
- Onion, red
- ½ tsp of sesame oil
- ½ tsp of yuzu juice or lime juice
- 1 teaspoon of mirin
- 1 teaspoon of soy sauce
- ½ avocado, ripe
- Nori blatt (green mat - crispy seaweed)
- 1 pinch of smoked salt, danish
- Chili

PREPARATION

Total time approx. 20 minutes

1. Clean the fish and fry briefly on the skin side.

2. Prepare the vegetables: Cut the red onion into thin slices. The spring onion in fine strips. Cut the avocado into 1 cm cubes. Mix the sesame oil, yuzu juice, soy sauce and mirin for the marinade.

3. Cut the fried fish into bite-sized pieces and marinate briefly with the avocado and marinade.

4. Fill two bowls with 150 g of sushi rice each, put the finely chopped red onions on top and spread the marinated fish and the avocados on top. Decorate with a little spring onion and thin strips of crispy seaweed ("green mat"). If you want, you can add some chili for the hotness.

BBQ ROLLS

INGREDIENTS FOR 4 PORTIONS

- 12 discs of bacon
- 500 g of ground beef
- 2 teaspoons of salt
- 2 teaspoons of pepper
- 1 teaspoon of paprika powder, sweet
- 1 teaspoon of paprika powder, spicy
- 1 tbsp of barbecue sauce for ground beef
- 4 chili pepper (jalapenos)
- 1 piece of cheese
- 1 bottle of barbecue sauce to spread on
- ½ bag of nacho

PREPARATION

Total time approx. 1 hour 30 minutes

1. Season the ground beef according to taste with salt, pepper, paprika powder and barbecue sauce. Place twelve slices of baron overlapping on the sushi mat and spread the ground beef evenly over the bacon. Halve, core and place the jalapenos in the middle of the minced meat. Place the strips of cheese on the jalapenos. Roll everything up with the help of the sushi mat.

2. Briefly fry the roll in oil and then put it in the oven at 200 degrees. Brush the roll from time to time with the barbecue sauce and turn it over so that it turns brown on all sides.

3. Crumble the nachos and roll the fried roll in the nacho crumbs, cut open and serve.

ASIAN FISH BALLS

INGREDIENTS FOR 1 PORTIONS

- 1 can of tuna in its own juice
- 2 teaspoons of wasabi paste
- 3 tsp of mayonnaise
- 1 teaspoon of pickled ginger (sushi ginger)
- 1 teaspoon of soy sauce
- 2 tbsp of sesame

PREPARATION

Total time approx. 10 minutes

1. Process all ingredients except for the sesame in a food processor to a homogeneous mass. Form 12 small balls out of the mass and roll them in sesame. Place on a plate and serve with ginger and wasabi.

DESSERT

SUSHI WITH A DIFFERENCE - SWEET AS A DESSERT

INGREDIENTS FOR 6 PORTIONS

- 200 g of rice pudding
- 1 liter of milk
- 1 pinch of salt
- 5 tbsp of sugar
- Vanilla bean
- 100 g of grated coconut
- Mango, ripe
- 200 g of strawberries
- 8 kiwi
- Fruit for decoration

PREPARATION

Total time approx. 1 hour

1. First prepare the rice pudding according to the package instructions with sugar, salt, milk and scraped-out vanilla pulp, it should be sticky and not too firm. While the rice pudding is cooking, grate the grated coconut in a pan over medium heat without fat until it is fragrant and golden brown.

2. Then you wash and cut the fruit. The strawberries are cut into thin slices. 6 kiwi fruit and three quarters of the mango are also cut into thin slices. The milk rice cams are later topped with this fruit.

3. The rest of the mango and the remaining kiwis are cut lengthways so that thicker stripes are created that are as long as possible. These will later be used to fill the sushi rolls.

4. The best way to shape the rice pudding when it is still warm is to let it cool down briefly until it is easy to touch. First you cover a sushi mat (works without it, but it is a little trickier) with transparent film and sprinkle it thickly in the form of a rectangle with the toasted coconut flakes. Width about 10 cm, length as desired and length of the sushi mat. Then spread the rice pudding carefully with the help of a knife. Now place the kiwi and mango strips in the middle of the rice pudding, then roll up the roll carefully using the mat and the transparent film. Everything should be firmly pressed on. Make 2 rolls in this way. Now rest the rolls in the fridge and let them harden.

5. Form the remaining rice pudding into cams with the help of two tablespoons and arrange them on a plate. Cover the cams with the strawberry, kiwi and mango slices.

6. Take the sushi rolls out of the refrigerator and carefully cut them into slices with a sharp knife and arrange them on the plates as well.

7. Can now be decorated with more fruit.

SWEET SUSHI

INGREDIENTS FOR 2 PORTIONS

- Carrot
- Apples
- 250 g of strawberries
- 100 g of pistachios, finely ground
- Mango
- 1 bar of leek
- 250 g of rice for sushi
- 1 liter of milk
- 100 g of sugar
- Vanilla bean
- Orange, the grated peel of it
- Lemon, the grated peel of it
- 4 nori sheets
- 250 ml of maple syrup
- 20 g of crème fraiche cheese
- 40 g of sugar
- Ginger, candied, for garnish

PREPARATION

Total time approx. 45 minutes

1. First boil the rice with the milk, the vanilla pod, the sugar, the orange peel and the lemon peel. Cover and let swell at the edge of the hearth for approx. To cool, spread flat on a large baking sheet and chill.

2. Now prepare various rolls as follows:

3. Maki with carrot and apple (2 rolls)

4. Peel the carrot, grate finely, add a little sugar and drizzle with a little lemon juice. Peel the apples, cut them into rectangular pens of the same size and acidify them slightly with lemon juice. Place the rice on a bamboo mat, place a nori sheet on top and press down a little.

5. Spread rice on the algae leaf and line up the apple sticks 2 cm from the lower edge parallel to the edge. Roll up the sushi roll firmly, loosening the rice from the mat. Then roll in the carrot grated.

6. Maki with strawberries and pistachio (2 rolls)

7. As described above, only use strawberries instead of apples and 100 g pistachios instead of carrots.

8. Nigiri with mango and sweet leek (8 pieces)

9. Cut 8 rice nocks and shape them by hand. Peel the mango and cut the largest possible pieces. Cut 8 slices of the size of the rice noodles into a rectangle and place them on the rice nocks. Wash 2 large leek leaves, briefly brew in very sweet boiling water and quench in ice water. Cut fine green strips from it and wrap the sushi with them.

Pistachio cream:

1. Puree the pistachios, crème fraiche and sugar in the blender.

2. Arrange the sushi rolls on plates and garnish with the candied ginger. Maple syrup and pistachio cream are enough.

SWEET SUSHI WITH FRUITS

INGREDIENTS FOR 4 PORTIONS

- 150 g of rice (sushi or risotto rice)
- 100 ml of water
- 150 ml of milk
- 4 tbsp of sugar
- Vanilla bean
- Kiwi
- 100 g of mango
- Strawberries
- 3 tbsp of apricot jam
- 3 tbsp of cocoa powder, unsweetened

PREPARATION

Total time approx. 30 minutes

1. Place the rice in a sieve and wash until the water becomes clear. Put rice in a saucepan with 100 ml of water, milk and sugar. Halve the vanilla pod, scrape out the pulp, add to the rice and bring to the boil. Reduce the heat and simmer the rice for about 20 minutes, stirring often. Only when the liquid is completely absorbed, put the rice in a bowl and let it cool.

2. Peel the kiwi and mango and cut into strips. Clean and quarter the strawberries. Cut two strips of cling film into rectangles measuring approx. 20 cm x 15 cm and lay them flat on the work surface.

3. Spread the rice over the two pieces of transparent film and spread out into two rectangles. Press the rice down a bit and spread the apricot jam on the rice surface. Distribute the fruit as strips in the lower third of the rice. Using the foil, beat the rice over the fruits and form a roll. Remove the sushi rolls from the foil and roll them carefully into cocoa powder. Then cut into slices and serve.

RICE PUDDING

INGREDIENTS FOR 1 PORTIONS

- 250 g of rice (sushi rice)
- 100 ml of milk
- 250 ml of water
- 4 tbsp of honey
- 100 g of peanuts, unsalted, finely chopped
- 100 g of raspberries
- Powdered sugar for sprinkling
- Compote of your choice

PREPARATION

Total time approx. 30 minutes

1. Wash rice with cold water. Then put in a saucepan with the milk and water for about 20 minutes and bring to the boil. Then cover and let swell for about 15 minutes.

2. Sweet rice with honey and divide into 2 portions. Cover a sushi mat with cling film. Approx. Sprinkle half of the area with half of the chopped peanuts. Spread a portion of rice finger-thick on top, press firmly and press in a hollow in the middle of the length. Add half of the raspberries. Roll the rice into a firm roll using the mat.

3. Prepare a second roll from the remaining rice, peanuts and raspberries. Cool the rolls wrapped in cling film for about 2 hours.

4. Cut each roll into 6 pieces (the best way to do this is to leave the rice in the cling film, otherwise it will crumble easily - only remove the cling film afterwards).

5. Sprinkle with powdered sugar and arrange with compote.

BANANA MAKI SUSHI

INGREDIENTS FOR 1 PORTIONS

- Banana
- Tortilla, Mexican
- Nutella

PREPARATION

Total time approx. 5 minutes

1. Brush a tortilla with Nutella, roll the peeled banana into it. Cut the roll into maki pieces about 3 cm wide.

2. Arrange on a plate and garnish with strawberries.

SUMMER SUSHI

INGREDIENTS FOR 10 PORTIONS

- 100 g of Sushi rice or milk rice
- 200 ml of Coconut milk
- 2 tbsp of Sweetener of choice, e.g. Rice syrup, cane sugar, xylitol...
- Fruits of your choice, e.g. Banana, melon...

PREPARATION

Total time approx. 2 hours 5 minutes

1. Wash the sushi rice. Then put in a saucepan with 150 ml coconut milk and simmer with the lid on over medium heat. It took me about 15-20 minutes.

2. Remove from the stove and let it steep for another 5 minutes. Then let the rice cool completely. Then stir in the remaining coconut milk.

3. Take some rice in your hand, form small sausages or balls and place on a plate. Cut the fruit elongated, lay it on top and press it down.

SUSHI CAKE

INGREDIENTS FOR 1 PORTIONS

- 300 g of sushi rice
- 5 nori sheets
- 200 g of cream cheese
- Cucumber
- 400 g of salmon fillet (2 pieces of 200 g each)
- Avocado
- Sesame
- Pickled ginger
- Wasabi
- Soy sauce

PREPARATION

Total time approx. 2 hours 30 minutes

1. Cook the sushi rice according to the package and then process it with rice vinegar, salt and sugar to create the typical sushi rice. Then let the rice cool down a bit.

2. Peel the cucumber. Peel and stone avocados. Cut the cucumber, avocados and salmon fillets into slices.

3. Line the bottom of a 26-inch spring form tin with cling film and then clamp the edge back on.

4. Add an approx. Thumb-thick or, depending on your taste, thick / thin layer of sushi rice and press flat. Tilt this bottom onto a round cake plate. Now spread a thick layer of cream cheese on the rice soil, then put the nori sheets on top. Just cut it so that everything is covered. Spread salmon, avocado and cucumber on top. If the cake has to stand a little, simply drizzle lemon on the avocado, otherwise it will turn brown. Immediately put the bottom in the fridge because of the fish.

5. Create a second base with the remaining sushi rice using a new layer of cling film in the spring form pan. Spread this in the spring form pan with a thick layer of cream cheese and then put the nori sheets on top. Now carefully tip the second floor onto the first floor.

6. Now you can decorate: sesame, the remaining nori leaves, wasabi, ginger and leftover ingredients. The imagination knows no limits.

7. Use a very sharp or serrated knife to cut and slowly cut carefully. Makes 12 pieces.

8. Serve with the pickled ginger, wasabi and soy sauce. Best to eat with a knife and fork.

CUCUMBER SUSHI

INGREDIENTS FOR 25 PORTIONS

- 75 g of sushi rice
- 1½ tbsp of rice vinegar
- ¼ tsp of salt
- ¾ tsp of sugar
- 1 large cucumber
- 2 teaspoons of wasabi paste
- 150 g of smoked salmon (slices)
- 20 g of caviar
- 1 bed of cress

PREPARATION

Total time approx. 30 minutes

1. Wash the rice in standing cold water, drain on a sieve. Repeat the process until the water remains clear. Put the rice with 100 ml of cold water in a saucepan and let it rest for about 20 minutes. Close the pan tightly, bring the contents to a boil over high heat, let swell for approx. 10 minutes on very mild heat. Take the pan off the stove, put a folded tea towel between the pan and the lid, let it swell for about 10 minutes.

2. Lightly heat rice vinegar, salt and sugar in a small saucepan until the sugar has dissolved. Put the rice in a large bowl and mix in the vinegar thoroughly. Let the rice cool down.

3. Peel the cucumber (leave a few peel strips at will), halve lengthways and core. Spread wasabi paste on the inside of the cucumber halves. Pour rice into the cucumber halves. Cut the salmon into short strips.

4. Cut the filled cucumber halves diagonally into 2–3 cm wide pieces. Put some smoked salmon and caviar on each. Garnish with cress as you like.

Printed in Great Britain
by Amazon